D1593807

Jack Dempsey

JACK DEMPSEY

by

NAT FLEISCHER

ARLINGTON HOUSE NEW ROCHELLE, NEW YORK

All photographs courtesy of *The Ring Magazine.*

Library of Congress Catalog Card Number 72-78480

ISBN 0-87000-151-5

MANUFACTURED IN THE UNITED STATES OF AMERICA

To my loving daughter

JOAN LOUBET

Foreword

No man was as well qualified as Nat Fleischer to write this book about Jack Dempsey. No writer could bring to this happy task a greater knowledge of Jack as a boxer, a world champion, and an idol of the fight public, and keener insights into the Manassa Mauler's career.

Nat Fleischer, publisher of *The Ring* magazine, the world's outstanding boxing publication, which this year, 1972, celebrates its fiftieth anniversary, faced his typewriter with a thorough knowledge of Dempsey's apprenticeship, his years as the world heavyweight king, his two encounters with Gene Tunney.

Fleischer's memories reach across the long bridge of years to Jack's first appearances in New York, to that rainy night in Philadelphia on which the Mauler lost his title to Tunney, to the return match in Chicago a year later, which saw Jack beaten by the ex-marine, despite Tunney's trip to the canvas for the famous "long count." And those memories come alive herein.

In this book, about Kid Blackie, as Jack was called when he broke into boxing, about Mine Host, as he is today, Fleischer writes about the Mauler not only as a fighter, but also as a most interesting out-of-the-ring character, a social entity, and a partner-at-arms with the crafty Jack Kearns, who managed him into the title.

In short, this book is the best yet written on William Harrison Dempsey.

DAN DANIEL

August 1972

Preface

THIS is my second book about Jack Dempsey, fistic hero, one-time heavyweight champion of the world, and outstanding figure in the history of modern pugilism.

My first book was almost exclusively biographical, devoted virtually in its entirety to his work in the ring. This volume captures Dempsey the man as well as Dempsey the fighter, and brings the story up to date. I've also tried to make my approach more anecdotal.

I had a lot of fun writing it, setting down recollections which involved not only Jack, but myself too. I found myself rolling back the years and seeing Jack as a title aspirant, as a champion, as the victor over Jess Willard, as the two-time loser to Gene Tunney.

I found myself back in the Golden Days, the days of Tex Rickard and his genius for successful boxing promotion, with Dempsey as his ace performer.

I harked back to the dramatic days of the bizarre and incredible Jack Kearns, who did so much to make Dempsey the champion, but who could not agree with the champion in matters of essential importance. Between Kearns and Dempsey came the beautiful Estelle Taylor, who became Mrs. Jack Dempsey. She broke up the partnership.

I hope the reader matches the pleasure I experienced in writing this book.

Nat Fleischer

April 1972

1

JACK DEMPSEY celebrated his 75th birthday on June 24, 1970. Of all the tributes that came pouring in at this time, none was more memorable than the one received a week earlier in the ring at Madison Square Garden. The feature attraction was a heavyweight contest between Jerry Quarry and Mac Foster, but the hero of the evening turned out to be the old Manassa Mauler, still the Idol of Fistiana at age 75.

Special ceremonies honoring Dempsey swelled the attendance for the boxing show to 15,915, causing John F. X. Condon, Madison Square Garden's energetic boxing public relations director, to comment wistfully, "Maybe Dempsey can have another birthday next month."

It was indeed a night for thrills and nostalgia. Shown on two giant screens was a special film of Dempsey's epic battles with Jess Willard, Luis Angel Firpo, and Gene Tunney. Then came the grand array.

Georges Carpentier, the Orchid Man, whom Manassa Jack had knocked out in four rounds at Boyle's Thirty Acres in Jersey City on July 2, 1921, in the first contest to draw a million-dollar gate, came from France to honor his old foe. Jack Sharkey, stopped by Dempsey in 1927 in the battle Jack had to win to get another shot at Tunney, the man who had taken the title from him, came down from New Hampshire. Tunney, twice conqueror of Dempsey, and hero—or villain (depending on how you look at it)—of the "long count," climbed through the ropes as the crowd roared, to greet the Manassa Mauler.

Then, as the rafters reverberated, the honored guest himself acknowledged the tribute to him in the center of the ring. Current heavyweight titleholder Joe Frazier, on behalf of the Garden, presented the old Manassa Mauler with an oil painting of himself and a desk set.

Also brought into the ring to honor Dempsey were such outstanding ringmen of the past and present as Paul Berlenbach, Mickey Walker, Willie Pep, Sandy Saddler, Carlos Ortiz, Dick Tiger, Jake LaMotta, Emile Griffith, Lou Salica, Phil Terranova, Jose Torres, George Chuvalo, Ben Jeby, Joey Giardello, Petey Scalzo, and Ismael Laguna. 'Twas truly a night to remember. But, then again, didn't Dempsey give millions upon millions of fans many other nights to remember during his brilliant fistic career?

To cap off Jack's 75th anniversary, he was called to City Hall to receive the Bronze Medallion of the city of New York from Mayor John V. Lindsay.

Jack Dempsey, even at 75, still ruled the imagination as to what a prizefighter should be. He was powerful, exciting, and dramatic. He typified strength. His dynamic left hook crashing against an opponent's chin was the pinnacle of knockout blows.

He was truly one of the Golden People of sports in the Golden Decade, the 1920s, along with Babe Ruth, Red Grange, Knute Rockne, Gertrude Ederle, Johnny Weissmuller, Bill Tilden, Tex Rickard, Bobby Jones, Helen Wills, Ty Cobb, and Gene Tunney—that immortal group which has been placed on Olympian pedestals.

Dempsey is still worshipped by the youth of America. Walking down the street he is likely to be mobbed; feminine hearts flutter in his presence; joyous acclaim greets him wherever he goes. The old magic still clings to him as in days of yore, long after his retirement.

It was always that way with Dempsey. Whenever he entered a crowded room, suddenly there seemed to be no one there but Jack Dempsey. Even if other well-known personalities or celebrities were there, they faded into insignificance, once Dempsey's presence became known.

And that spectacular dynamic something called charisma still clings to this day. Who can explain it? Yet Dempsey possesses it to the nth degree.

He was unquestionably the boxer of his era, perhaps the boxer of all eras. He dominated the game as villain, hero, and elder statesman as no one before or after has ever done.

Advancing from a hobolike existence to the highest peak in pugilism, his story is in truth a rags-to-riches saga. Only once, in his break with his manager Jack Kearns, did Dempsey lose sight of those who helped make it possible for him to achieve the heavyweight championship and the fortune he accumulated.

There were numerous obstacles Jack had to overcome in his climb to fame. They turned out to be insignificant, however, compared to the battle he waged to clear his name of draft-dodging attacks in World War I. Exonerated by a jury in 1920, the attitude of his besmirchers slowly changed to admiration as the years went by. Today, Dempsey enjoys international popularity and is an honored citizen the world over.

Few champions in any sport have been admired so universally. There are always a cheer and a handshake for him. He remains the everlasting monarch to the fans.

People of prominence greet him and express surprise at his ease, self-reliance, and assurance. He has a warm smile and sense of humor that endear him to all.

Dempsey is a good mixer. Since his retirement as a boxer and referee, Jack has absorbed a considerable amount of worldly knowledge, thus enabling the former mucker of mines to become the well-groomed man of dignity at ease anywhere, even at the White House where he has been a guest on several occasions.

I could write reams of praise of other fighting men such as Joe Louis, Rocky Marciano, Tommy Loughran, Jimmy Braddock, Benny Leonard, Barney Ross, Tony Canzoneri, Jack Sharkey, Willie Pep, and Tony Zale, to name only a few. In analyzing the field of modern fistic celebrities, however, I find that no pugilist surpasses Manassa Jack in public appeal and adulation.

His power attack and speed drew him to the public. When the bell clanged, a tiger was unleashed who went all out with flailing fists and a bewildering assortment of powerful punches possessed by very few.

Jack's undying gift to his craft was the influence he had in gaining public support for boxing following his second defeat at the hands of Tunney, a period that saw boxing go into a decline. Earlier, Dempsey was the principal factor in bringing boxing out of chaos after World War I.

Jack was not a scientific boxer, but a Fighter with a capital F—the slugger par excellence.

Tunney, Louis, Loughran, and Sharkey were more clever but the Manassa Mauler was power personified.

His was one of the first successful American sports sagas. He has been one of the most influential sports heroes of all time—a genuine he-man, big-hearted, kind, and generous, perhaps to a fault.

Jack Dempsey is the kind of man who comes along all too seldom.

2

THE MANASSA MAULER, William Harrison Dempsey, was born on June 24, 1895, the ninth child of a brood of eleven. His birthplace was in Manassa (Conejos County), Colorado, a Morman settlement. There were sisters Effie, Florence, Stella, Elsie, and Alice; brothers Joseph, John, Bruce, Robert, and Bernie. The last named, who decided on a boxing career, called himself Jack, the name the Manassa Mauler assumed after his brother quit the ring. Bruce, the baby of the family, was stabbed to death in 1917, at the age of 16.

William Harrison Dempsey's father, Hyrum, hailed from hardy stock. His ancestors had come from county Kildare, Ireland. Manassa Jack's fighting spirit and his love for the outdoors are traced to the Irish and Indian blood coursing through his veins.

Hyrum married Celia Smoot of Logan County, Colorado, a member of the famous Smoot clan. She was the second cousin of Reed Smoot, U.S. senator from Utah.

Celia Dempsey followed the bloodlines of the Scots and Irish on her father's side and those of the Cherokee Indian on her mother's. Her mother was half-Indian.

Both Celia and Hyrum were converts to the Morman faith. To this day, Jack lists himself as a member of that religion, although his children are Roman Catholics.

In 1931 Hyrum Dempsey married Hanna L. Chapman. Previously he and Celia were divorced.

Hyrum died in a Salt Lake City hospital, February 24, 1948, at 91. Advanced old age was given as the cause. Celia died in 1946.

At one time there was an effort to discover Jewish lines in Jack's family history. The attempt was in vain. However, two of his four wives have Jewish biographies—the late Hannah Williams of the Broadway stage, and the current Mrs. Dempsey, Deanna Piatelli, who was reared in Italy.

Manassa Jack's granddaddy, known as "Big Dempsey," was dubbed the Goliath of East Tennessee. The history of the Dempsey clan indicates that "Big Dempsey" was quite a heavyweight battler. His fame as a fistic expert spread throughout the mountains. Many mountaineers were eager to test the fighting skill of the husky, battling Dempsey. But, like Jess Willard and Georges Carpentier of later days, the mountaineers returned home saddened, humbled, aware that they didn't match the power, speed, stamina, and strength of "Big Dempsey."

Mother Celia can probably be credited with sparking Jack's burning desire to be a prizefighter, by her continual praise of John L. Sullivan. It seems that about three months before Jack was born, Celia Dempsey was alone in her mountain cabin on a cold, stormy night.

A peddler happened by and asked for shelter. Feeling sorry for the stranger, Celia gave him a warm place to sleep and a hot meal the next morning. To show his gratitude, the peddler told her to take anything she wanted from his wares. She refused, but he was so insistent that she finally picked out a book called *Life of a 19th Century Gladiator* by John L. Sullivan.

She read the book and gained great respect and affection for Sullivan. Then, the story goes, when little Harry, as Jack was called by his family, was old enough to understand such things, his mother told him all about the great John L.

According to some oldtimers around the Manassa area, young Harry was a quiet boy, strongly devoted to his mother. He was specially fond of little animals and birds. A born athlete, he was a standout in a number of sports, including the "sport" of fistfighting. Early he learned how to use his fists, and to use them well. But unlike many with fistic prowess, Harry never played the bully.

At the age of eight, little Harry was baptized into the Morman church. Dempsey recalls: "When I was a boy, the only thing I read was the Bible. When I became a professional boxer, I used to pray many times before a fight. I have always felt that religion and a person's beliefs are the most important things in life."

The Dempseys were extremely poor when Jack was a boy. In fact, he remembers not eating a piece of sugar candy until he was 15. And he recalls never owning a toy. But these days proved effective training for the lean times still to come.

Try as Hyrum Dempsey might, though he moved his large family around rather frequently, he could never seem to earn an adequate living. It was Celia who helped make ends meet by running a boardinghouse in Wagon Wheel Gap, Colorado, and later a restaurant at Montrose, a railroad town in the western part of the state.

Jack recalls these tough, hard boyhood days: "We ate poorly, had very few clothes, and worked too hard. I fed pigs, chopped wood, worked in the sugar beet fields, shined shoes in barbershops, helped pitch circus tents and move heavy equipment, and even shoveled dung. But, all in all, I don't regret having grown up that way. It made me tough and well prepared for the life ahead. I was never ill or down with sickness. My body became tough as leather." He also did his share of plowing, reaping, and sowing.

Dempsey, despite his heavy load of chores, made time for the joys of the outdoors. Once familiar with a gun, he in no time became an expert shot. His reputation as a skillful hunter and trapper, and as a good fisherman, was unquestioned.

In 1902, when Jack was about seven, the Dempsey brood moved from Manassa to Creede, a little mining town about 85 miles away, on the edge of the Great Divide.

The next stop was Uncompahgre, Colorado, about 175 miles

west of Manassa. It should have taken the Dempseys not more than two or three weeks to reach this town. It took them about two years. They traveled the long way around, stopping here and there for days and weeks at a time. One of their more extended stops was in Delta, Colorado, in 1904. But this same year they at last arrived at Uncompahgre, not far from Montrose.

It was during this journey that Celia Dempsey became seriously ill. After spending some time with Jack's sister, Florence, in Denver, her health returned. She rejoined the family in Steamboat Springs, Colorado.

At Uncompahgre Hyrum Dempsey got a job as a share rancher, working a place called the Albrush Ranch. Jack became a real-life working cowboy. But those comparatively happy days lasted for only a year. The Dempseys then became sharecroppers for a time, until Mama Dempsey decided to open in Montrose a hash house, which she called the Rio Grande Eating House. Jack, now about eleven, learned the dishwashing trade, and also did some waiting on tables. In addition to these duties, he shined shoes and sold newspapers and magazines.

It was around this time that William Harrison Dempsey began seriously to consider the possibility of fighting for a living. John L. Sullivan he knew about. But now he had a new hero—brother Bernie. Mainly through Bernie's instruction young Harry learned the rudiments of how to use his abundant fistic talent, of which he was becoming increasingly aware. And with this instruction, young Harry could see a new way of life, a life that before now had been but a glimmer on the horizon.

It is doubtful if the Dempseys knew anything about the great Nonpareil Jack Dempsey (no relative), onetime middleweight champion. He was the original Jack Dempsey who fought between 1883 and 1895. Death claimed him in 1895, shortly before his 33rd birthday, in Portland, Oregon.

In 1908 the Dempsey family picked up its meager belongings and moved to Provo, Utah, 40 miles south of Salt Lake City. Now 13, young Harry continued earning money any way he could—shining shoes, working beet fields, cleaning up barbershops, working in the mines.

Here also he continued his schooling, a bit more regularly than had been the case before now. From his very first day in school, Jack had never gone into ecstasy over having to attend classes. Studies and Jack just never meshed. Not that he was a poor student. He wasn't. He was just average, no better, no worse than most other healthy American boys his age, growing up in the West in an exciting era, when there was so much to do. True, he had had a somewhat difficult time of it in the Uncompahgre and Montrose schools, but much of the problem lay in the uncertainty of the Dempsey lot. What with Papa Dempsey traveling hither and yon with all the brood, it was ofttimes a man-sized chore to keep up with the books.

Jack did take a fancy to arithmetic, though. Besides doing well in that subject, there was something about working with figures that could hold his attention. But as for the rest of his studies, well he'd rather be out playing or, later on, hunting—or reading the *Police Gazette,* to savor the generous portion of boxing news in it.

But, finally, in June 1911, a few days before his 16th birthday, young Jack graduated from the eighth grade of the Lakeview school in Provo. And no sooner was the school door closed than he decided it was time to leave home and stake out his own claim in life. His few possessions secured and his goodbyes over, Jack left Provo—with $1.50 in his pocket.

3

WHEN YOUNG DEMPSEY left home that June of 1911, he started a roving life that had no end until he had won the world heavyweight crown. Although this commenced a new stage in his life, the odd jobs continued, albeit on a higher plane—ditch-digging, bouncer in dance halls, pick-and-shovel help in coal mines, leader in copper mines, or whatever came his way and he could do. He also engaged in an occasional fight. Freight cars often were his sleeping quarters.

He mingled with plain drifters, panhandlers, and professional men gone lush. This sort of living hardened the Manassa Mauler for the tough life he was to encounter on his way to New York and points East and West.

Sitting in his New York restaurant recently, he laughed when he recalled the many adventures in his days of adversity.

"My fighting career really got started when I was a drifter. You had to be alert, ready to protect yourself. If it weren't for the life I was leading then, I doubt my professional career would have gotten under way."

Dempsey's life story is divided into several cycles. Few of our other famous pugilists, except for John L. Sullivan, figured as much in the public eye as Jack.

A roving life, a preliminary fighter during which he encountered all the hardships that fall to the lot of boxing unknowns, a champion with glory and wealth, a promoter capitalizing on his magnetism, a popular restaurateur—through these stages Dempsey traveled and Dempsey prospered.

Talk to Dempsey about his days as a boxcar hobo, and he'll delight in reciting his experiences.

Take him back to the days when starvation faced him in Philadelphia, and he'll recount his travail with a smile.

Discuss his thrilling fights and you'll find him right at home.

These areas in the life of the Manassa Mauler arouse his memories, his nostalgia, his delight—and his regrets.

Thrown on his own resources as he matured, Dempsey made his way through the West via the freight-car route. A coach was an unknown comfort. Today he thinks little of crisscrossing the continent via air to visit his daughters and grandchildren in Hollywood, California.

On occasion, stories have appeared stating that articles on Dempsey's early life and travels around the West are untrue. Invariably the yarns are referred to as a buildup.

One story in particular, published in a Buffalo paper in 1930, brought a quick answer in the form of a two-column article by Damon Runyon, noted New York journalist, in which Damon refuted a story by Charley Murray, sports editor, that Dempsey never rode the beams. The story objected to by Runyon, follows:

"When Jack Dempsey came East under the management of Jack Kearns, the latter, for window dressing purposes, informed Runyon that his fighter had been a hobo. The blackness of his jowls was not hirsute, but imbedded layers of cinders contracted on the brake rods, blind baggage and top decks of railroad trains.

"The boy had travelled al fresco so long, that only close surveillance on the trip from San Francisco prevented Dempsey from slipping out of their Pullman compartment and playing peek-a-boo with the trainman under the coaches. Runyon made it a good story. I know that I took it for granted."

Runyon, upset by Murray's piece, answered it in the *New York Journal:*

"The truth of the matter is that I met Dempsey when he came to New York City for the first time in 1916, more than a year before Doc Kearns had ever heard of him. Dempsey had journeyed in from the West, sleeping in the same berth with Fat Jack Price, a pal from Utah, who was acting as Jack's manager. Jack fought Wild Bert Kenny, Andre Anderson and John Lester Johnson in New York, meantime going under the management of John the Barber Reisler, though Dempsey had previously signed a contract with Auerbach in Utah, a contract Dempsey later bought back for $5,000.

"After the Johnson fight, Dempsey severed relations with John the Barber and returned West. In that return, Jack rode the decks of passenger trains part of the way.

"I am not saying that riding the decks of a passenger train makes a man a hobo, but it surely doesn't make him a paying customer. Dempsey, on his own say-so, has given proof that he did a lot of traveling that way in his early days as a fighter.

"It was in 1917 that Dempsey tangled up with Kearns, and when he came East again, with Kearns as his mentor, it was with the name and fame of the most promising young heavyweight in the world.

"After Dempsey had won the championship, I said something to him about hoboing. He looked at me with disgust.

" 'I was no tramp, Damon,' he said. 'That was all ballyhoo. In the West, where fares were five cents a mile and distances were great, workmen often beat their way and I did it three times, possibly a few more, as a kid. But I never stole rides on freight trains.'

"Well, after Dempsey won the world title, and following his defeat of Georges Carpentier, we were on our way to Europe. Jack turned to me and said:

" 'Damon, let's forget that hobo business now. We want to be gentlemen after this.'

"Meaning of course, that he wanted to be so depicted.

"If Murray has any more doubts about the hobo story, he may be surprised to know that I have witnesses who ate with Jack out of tin cans and rode with Dempsey on freight trains. Jack was mighty proud of his rough, rod-riding career at the time.

"*A Tale of Two Fists* was written by me, and anyone who has travelled around the country with Dempsey as I have, and seen the weird characters that bob up on him in every town, mumbling of the old days and old experiences, knows Jack couldn't have met them in drawing rooms."

That's the story published by Damon Runyon in the *New York Journal* many years ago in answer to the charge that the Dempsey hobo yarn was untrue.

Jack Price, who was one of Dempsey's boxcar companions, told me this story of the discovery of Dempsey when he still was in his teens and riding the freight cars.

"I was young and foolish and at the time I met Jack, had a considerable fortune, at least considered so by my pals. It was money given to me by my guardian when I came of age according to a will in which I was named. It was my 21st birthday and I decided to celebrate.

"I showed the boys of Cripple Creek, Colorado, a good time. The next morning when I awoke, I found to my surprise that I had spent close to $2,000 around the saloons and gambling joints.

"In the evening, two friends and I decided to leave for Springfield, in southeastern Colorado. There we learned that jobs were open at $3.00 per day in Tucker, Utah. We decided to make the trip, but after three days, during which we worked practically for nothing, we quit and headed for the gold mines of Cripple Creek to work as muckers.

"We caught a freight train that evening and some hours later we landed in Green River, Utah. There we met a big, overgrown kid with bushy hair and staring eyes, lying on a pile of lumber. He was glad to see us.

" 'Where are you heading?' he asked.

" 'Down to Victor, Colorado, where the big mines of Cripple Creek are.'

" 'Probably you know my brother. His name is Scar Face Jack Dempsey.

" 'Sure I know him!'

"Our newfound friend was elated. He asked if he could join us. The brother was none other than Bernie Dempsey, the oldest of the Dempsey boys. Later he became the night marshal.

" 'Well,' said the kid, 'he's my brother. From Salt Lake City. See, I can fight like him.'

"He put up his hands to illustrate his brother's pose.

"We broke the seal off the boxcar that was full of sacked salt being shipped to Colorado Springs. There were several other hoboes in the vicinity and they all joined us.

"When we were part-way out, we made a stop and soon found ourselves in trouble with the railroad guards. One of them with a whip started swinging. A member of our group let go a blow that caught him on the chin and down he went. That was the signal for all of us to vacate our snug quarters.

"Shortly after, I took out my purse to see how much I had left and found that I had spent most of my dough carousing all night in one of the saloons prior to meeting Dempsey.

"I believe that was the last of Jack Dempsey's freight rides. He told me he never stole a ride on a freight train after that experience."

Otto Floto, a sports editor and a close friend of Jack's, told me a story about a holdup which belongs in the Dempsey saga.

"Dempsey asked me to handle his affairs after Jack had quit one of his many managers back in the teens before Kearns. We barnstormed through the West and picked up what we could. Things were pretty tough. We had little money between us.

"I had an old touring car. We had to fight three or four times a week to keep going, but we managed it. We got some work in the mining towns and picked up fights that don't appear in the record book because they never hit the newspapers. Now and then we were fortunate by hitting a packed house. Such was the case when we struck a Colorado town on a mine payday and the flush residents were in a mood for a fight.

"I got the promoter of a dance hall to put Jack on with a tough miner. Jack knocked him goofy in two rounds. Our purse reached the high figure of $600. That was a real payday.

"On our way to Grand Junction to spend the night, a car pulled along side of us on a narrow turn on a mountain road, and crowded our car against a rocky wall. Four men jumped out. One held a gun and ordered us to come out with hands up.

" 'This is a holdup. Don't move,' the gunman ordered.

"I had the $600 in a briefcase. I tossed the bag to the bandits and off the quartet went, with one still pointing his gun at us. It was a tough break. We had a few dollars left between us. There was nothing we could do but continue on our way to Grand Junction, nearly broke.

"We drove on and shortly arrived at the Grand Junction Hotel and Lunch Room which was open all night. Jack and I decided to get a sandwich prior to going to our room. As Jack was talking to the waiter, I turned to him and whispered, 'Jack, do you see what I see at the table in front of us?'

"I was crippled, having undergone a leg amputation and I didn't care to face those fellows again. But there were our bandits, enjoying a meal with our dough.

"They quickly recognized Jack, and got to their feet, preparing for action.

"So did Dempsey. He didn't waste any time. He sailed into the robbers. He hauled off at the nearest one, clouted him on the jaw and dropped him like a log. Three others followed.

"The one carrying the case with the money tossed it on the floor. Dempsey grabbed it, then went through the pockets of the thieves. He recovered all the money and confiscated the gun that had been pulled on us. He crashed his fist into the stomach of each of the highwaymen and tossed the men out on the road.

"Jack stood outside the door and as each robber regained his feet, Dempsey let go a parting warning.

" 'If you want more, come back,' he snarled.

"That was one of the fights not recorded in Manassa Jack's record."

Royal Brougham of Seattle, one of the many sportswriting friends of Dempsey, visited Jack in his New York restaurant after Dempsey had completed *The Jack Dempsey Story* for the movies.

"Will the film tell about the time you rolled into Seattle on a slow freight, patches in your pants, a three-day growth of beard and only $3.00 in your jeans?" asked the Seattle editor.

The champion laughed. "Sure, it makes an interesting part of my story. I told them to shoot the works—not to hold back anything."

"Those ragamuffin days will make an interesting episode in the picture," said Brougham.

"The hungry unknown fighter hunting for a meal and a bed in a flophouse; the rivet-tossing days and other interesting stories in the rise to world champion, are they all in the film?" asked Brougham.

"They sure are," replied Jack. "The film wouldn't be worth making if they were eliminated."

And they were right there in the film, nothing doctored for easy viewing.

Today little remains of the old mining days, the bearded, cinder-covered, roughnecked Dempsey riding the baggage cars from town to town, getting beaten up and dishing it out in Western style. The restlessness that was his is gone. Some of the scars remain, but little else to remind him of his early days when he was picking up a little change by tackling any opponent who would fill the bill with him in a dance hall or a tank-town boxing emporium.

He absorbed the ways of business. The pain, hunger, and hardships are things of the past. The tough dives of his younger days, the freight cars hurtling through the night, the clothesline ropes within which he fought, the blood-soaked gloves which he donned—they're all gone.

He never engaged in a boxing match when he faced an opponent. It was always a battle, like the bruising ones in which he engaged with Johnny Sudenberg in Goldfield and Tonopah, Nevada.

"When I was fighting my way up before Kearns took me in hand, I worked in a place called the Northern Bar," Dempsey related to me in discussing his early start as a fighter. "An Indian pug, Kid Harrison, was my sparmate. He had a terrific, stiff wallop, but he couldn't take a punch without squirming. I knocked him stiff one day and he quit the camp.

" 'You hit too hard,' he told me. 'I can't take 'em.'

"I then got the services of a chap named Roy Moore. He was

strong, durable, a fighter who could give and take a good punch. He gave me more good workouts than I got from the Indian.

"We worked together for the Sudenberg fight and he taught me some excellent points. The fights I had with Sudenberg and the rough workouts with Moore, made me the tough battler I had become in my early schooling, before I joined Kearns. Jungle camp brawls developed me into the vicious fighter I became. I owed a lot to Moore."

4

THE FIRST TIME Dempsey entered the promotion field was in 1913, before Manassa Jack had decided to make boxing his career. It was while working in a dance hall in the Moose Club in Montrose, California. He not only was one of the principals in a bout with Freddy Woods, but also handled the cash.

Dempsey and Freddy agreed to split the gate and each received $20. Dempsey told me that was more than he had received from John (the Barber) Reisler for engaging tough Andre Anderson in New York in ten rounds. For the New York battle, Dempsey's share was only $16.

About his fight with Woods, Dempsey, relating the story, remarked:

"I was a kid of only eighteen at the time and Woods and I worked in a blacksmith's shop. He had fought a few battles and was tough. I was a raw novice. They called him the 'Fighting Blacksmith.' He got to talking about some fights he had, and I became interested.

" 'Let's put on a show on Saturday night. We can get a few bucks,' I suggested. He accepted.

" 'We'll share the dough,' he said.

"Montrose had need for fistic entertainment and I quickly sold the idea. We got the hall free, put together a ring with clotheslines, sprinkled the floor with sawdust and were ready for action.

"I stood at the door and collected the dough," continued Jack. "When it was time for the fight to get under way, I hung up my trousers in which I had placed our money.

"When the gong sounded, we tore into each other. We wanted to please our friends from the mine. It was a knock-down, drag-out fight in which everything went. We often carved huge chunks out of the air, but we also missed some beauties and the crowd enjoyed it.

"In the second round, I clouted Freddy with a right to the jaw and he hit the floor. He got up on time and one of the boys tossed a bucket of water over him. When he recovered, he insisted on continuing. We had a tough time restraining him. He was in no condition to go on with the fight.

"I calmed him while holding him down in his chair. I whispered into his ear, 'You fool, we ain't fightin' for nothing. We're splitting the gate. We've got forty bucks between us. We can fight again in a couple of weeks.'

"The mention of forty bucks caused Freddy to toss his head back with a jerk. It was big money for each of us, and we left the fight scene quite satisfied."

It was in 1914 that Manassa Jack, flat broke, ran into Andy Malloy, a tough veteran, who like Jack was seeking help. He induced Dempsey to set up a fight for the pair. Malloy already had given Dempsey's brother a shellacking.

The night of the Dempsey-Malloy affair, Moose Hall was crowded with miners.

"They realized they would see good action," said Dempsey in recalling the affair. He fought Malloy under the name of Kid Blackie.

"It was a dingdong battle with plenty of punches tossed and a persistent attack keeping the fans on edge. I landed a right on Malloy's jaw and put him out. That victory was so unexpected that when Malloy came to, he remarked:

" 'Jack, you're too good to be riding the rods. Let me manage you. We both can make dough. What do you say?'

"Of course that appealed to me. All I wanted to do was to fight.

It was all I cared about. Malloy taught me how to throw my weight behind a punch. My first big piece of information—the follow through.

"It wasn't long after that Malloy got a message from Buck Weaver, a miner sportsman, offering to pair Malloy and me in Durango, Colorado, a good, lively mining locality. We broke our business partnership and accepted Weaver's offer.

"We went to Durango where we were booked at the Opera House for a ten-round bout. That was in 1914. The police came to the rescue of Malloy in the middle of the final round after he had received some stiff wallops. He then decided to hang up his gloves. My brother Bernie was satisfied by now that I was getting somewhere and he decided to take over as my manager."

Harry Downing, Salt Lake City promoter, after receiving a letter from Malloy informing him of the prowess of Dempsey, wired Jack an offer to fight Jack Downey in the Mormon metropolis. Manassa Jack accepted.

The fight took place April 5, 1915. It was a four-round match, with enough bloodletting for ten rounds. Jack lost the decision. It was a homicidal affair, he told me.

Now Dempsey was a restless young man who had turned from riding the rods to a profession he enjoyed, and in which he was making considerable progress. But the roving spirit soon got the better of the Manassa Mauler again. He went back to the mines. During this time he took on many opponents who are not listed in his fighting record.

The Golden Cycle, the Highland Coin, and the Victor were but a few of the dance halls that gave him opportunities to fight local miners and itinerant leather throwers. Although the Manassa Mauler's battles following his winning of the heavyweight title gained for Jack prestige and fortune, these early contests are the ones Dempsey likes best to discuss.

The greatest thrill he relives is his three bouts with Johnny Sudenberg, particularly the one in Goldfield, Nevada, July 1915. Here is Jack's recollection:

"The setting was a camp with a motley group of miners looking on. A few weeks earlier, Sudenberg and I fought a savage ten-rounder in Tonopah [Nevada], which I won. The memories of that battle were still fresh when I faced Johnny in a return encounter.

"It was a blistering day with the heat simmering over the sagebrush and sand. No cameras, no mikes. We were in a gory era, between bare knuckles and gloves, and our patrons came for action."

Dempsey hauled out an old newspaper clipping from his desk. "Here, Nat, read this. It's the story of the bout in a Nevada paper."

Here's the yarn as it appeared in the local press:

"The gong sounded. Dempsey rushed forth for what he had planned as a fast-finish killing. The fireworks started with a solid right landing on Sudenberg's chin. Then followed a right that came up from a low crouch and it crashed with telling effect against the chin of Jack's opponent.

"The punch lifted Dempsey's opponent off his feet. He turned a somersault and landed on his back.

"Up he jumped after the count had reached seven. Dempsey, the killer instinct aroused, crashed another right, this time almost up from the floor, and down went Sudenberg again. Four times more Manassa Jack put his man on the canvas, but each time Sudenberg returned to battle.

"To the astonishment of the miners, who got a great kick out of Dempsey's performance, when Sudenberg regained a fighting position following the last knockdown, he swung his left with power to Dempsey's jaw. The bell came to Jack's rescue.

"In the second round, Dempsey put his opponent down again several times, but he couldn't keep Johnny on the canvas. After the seventh knockdown, Sudenberg decided to change his tactics and make a running fight of it. That was not to Dempsey's liking.

"Sudenberg kept circling Jack and stabbing away with lefts to the face. That type of battling continued for three rounds. Then came the break in the seventh round.

"Sudenberg dashed out of his corner and instead of circling Jack, he decided on a toe-to-toe battle. He slugged away."

Dempsey interrupted my reading of the article and said, "Now I would like to continue the story.

"As Sudenberg let go his right, I stepped in quickly and

twice he floored me with power rights to the jaw. Each time I beat the count and rushed in at close range with a body attack but I couldn't keep Sudenberg down.

"During the remainder of the battle, I tossed everything I had at him, but he stood his ground and landed plenty of stinging blows, most of which struck my jaw and hurt. Johnny survived the punishment I dished out, kept on his feet, and lasted the distance. He, not I, received the applause, because of his gameness. I will say now, he deserved it.

"In the eighth round I went down from a right that landed with a thud on my jaw. Believe me, that blow hurt.

"It was the hardest I received in the early days of my career. Three times in that round he had me on the canvas. I can't to this day understand how I was able to get back on my feet.

"No sooner did I rise than, bang! another shot struck me with terrific force and down I went again. Johnny had suffered plenty of punishment in the earlier rounds, but surely was making up for it.

"We were both a mess when the final gong called a halt to our slugfest. We gave the crowd what they had come to see. They got their money's worth.

"He certainly handed me a shellacking as we reached the end. I didn't believe he had anything left, but he proved otherwise.

"The miners went wild. They hadn't expected to see such action. They were treated to a great, hard-hitting, thrilling battle.

"When the last gong clanged, I was overjoyed. I can't recall any time in my career that I was so happy to hear it. I was forced to the limit in that brawl, which was called a draw."

Another contest which Dempsey says he will never forget was that with the Boston Bearcat, a Negro whom Jack fought in the Alhambra Theater in Ogden, Utah, in 1916.

The burly, tough-looking Negro walked into the theater and asked to see the fight promoter. He explained that he was a fighter and was badly in need of work. He would tackle anyone the promoter would offer as an opponent.

In those days, the owner of the movie house usually was hooked up with several other ventures, among them fight promotions. So it was in this case.

"How do I know that you can fight? What's your ring record? What's your name and who did you last fight?" asked the promoter.

The visitor pulled from his pocket several clippings, one with the report of a six-round bout with Sam Langford.

The promoter took out his record book, hunted through the pages, but failed to find any reference in Sam's record to any such fight. In those days, however, records were not kept so accurately as they are today. The promoter took the word of the visitor, handed him two dollars, told him to go get something to eat, and asked him to return at four o'clock.

When the Negro left, the promoter got in touch with Dempsey and asked if he would be available for a session at his club the following Friday against a newcomer. Since Dempsey had stopped Two Round Gilhan in Salt Lake City a fortnight earlier, the promoter figured he would have a good drawing card.

"Who is the guy?" asked Dempsey.

"I never heard of him. He's a big black boy who says he went six rounds with Sam Langford. He looks rough, but I don't think you'll have any trouble. How about taking the fight?"

"Sure. Go ahead," said Dempsey.

On fight night a large delegation from Salt Lake City came to Ogden to see the affair.

"When they arrived," Dempsey recalled, "the fans were surprised that I'd take on such a husky opponent. For a time even the promoter feared the fight might have to be called off, because the black man had too big of an advantage over me. I told the promoter to go ahead. I was eager to get into action.

"When the gong sounded, I leaped in, clouted the giant with a right. He dropped his hands and stood looking at me bewildered. He didn't expect that I would strike so soon. He now was seeing gloves tossed from all angles—hooks, swings, straight clouts, and uppercuts.

"He suddenly decided to rush me. He swung a left, which I ducked. Another attempt also missed. I countered with a beauty to his chin that shook him up. The punch turned him around, then he went down with a thud.

"Now the real fun got under way. The referee started to count. He had already begun when my opponent raised his hand off the floor and shouted:

" 'No moh fightin'. I'se finished.'

"The crowd roared as the black man got to his feet and started to remove the gloves. I had knocked him out in slightly more than two minutes. That put me on solid ground with the fans."

It may be said with certainty that no champion has been so frank about his early difficulties.

5

SEVERAL OTHER HEAVYWEIGHTS of those days sought a shot at Jess Willard's heavyweight crown as fervently as did Dempsey. That's where the managerial genius of Jack Kearns came in handy. Although Dempsey lost twice to Gene Tunney in the twilight of Manassa Jack's career, his performances against Willard, Georges Carpentier, and Luis Firpo were among the most spectacular contests in fistic history.

What John L. Sullivan meant to boxing in the bare-knuckle days, Dempsey meant to the modern era. With a granite jaw and iron fists, Jack feared no man. After his tutelage under Kearns, Dempsey was not long gaining public attention as the number-one heavyweight contender.

Jack Kearns, a shrewd, cunning manager, plotted a future for Dempsey that clearly pointed to the world championship. He decided that the best way of achieving it was to force prominent contenders to accept Dempsey as an opponent or advertise their fear.

But before teaming up with Kearns, Dempsey embarked on

his first trip to New York City. The year was 1916. It was this trip, as much as anything else, that convinced Manassa Jack he needed experienced and reliable managerial direction—in short, a Kearns.

Dempsey one day reviewed for me some of the troubles he encountered in New York and the disillusionment that set in after having expected so much.

"Do you recall, Jack," I asked, "how angry you were when you were gypped by the promoter when you fought John Lester Johnson? I thought at the time you were getting ready for a battle with your manager for handing you only a fifth of the amount to which you were entitled. Did you ever get any more than the $100 after you bitterly complained?"

"Not a cent," replied Jack. "As you know I went through ten terrific rounds and fought with a broken rib from the second through the tenth. You can imagine how I felt to have my purse cut by $400.

"Here I had come to New York in the hopes of making a lot of dough and was rewarded with $150 for three fights, each a tough battle. In addition, I suffered a broken rib. Do you blame me for quitting New York after that?

"I did so well in the Johnson fight, made such a fine showing, that I was repaid in part for the loss of the dough. That last fight helped me considerably when I got back to California.

"Few people knew that I came to New York weighing only a little over 160 pounds, a green, inexperienced youngster. But I fought tough heavyweights, especially Johnson.

"I stood toe-to-toe with my opponent for ten rounds and took all he tossed at me, in spite of the broken rib that was pressing into my stomach and making things unbearable. Every time I breathed, I felt I was being stabbed with a sharp knife.

"When I think of that fight, I can shake hands with myself that I had sufficient grit and sand to stick it out under such circumstances. If I hadn't been gypped in the three fights I had in New York, I probably would have remained in the East. However, things turned out pretty well for me on the Pacific Coast."

A few days before turning over his management to John (the Barber) Reisler, Dempsey visited the office of the *New York Press,* of which I was the sports editor. I had a good interview with him and published it in the Sunday edition, the only New York newspaper in the country at the time that carried eight pages of sports each weekend. I wrote that Dempsey had knocked out 27 opponents in fights through the mining districts of the West and had come to New York in quest of action.

Three days after Jack's arrival in my office, Tom McArdle, matchmaker of Billy Gibson's Fairmont Athletic Club, with whom I had discussed Dempsey's visit and quest for an engagement in the East, signed Jack for a bout of ten rounds with Andre Anderson, a towering heavyweight with a good record.

"The kid," as McArdle called Dempsey, "may go four or five rounds with Andre. He doesn't look like a tough fighter, but we'll give him a try. If he does well, I can put him in at least one more bout."

Dempsey was pleased with the opportunity to show in New York. He told me he had dreamed of that chance quite frequently. He added that he told McArdle he wouldn't be disappointed. The bout took place on June 24, 1916.

The opening round with Anderson was a hectic one for Jack. No matter what he tried, he was outscored and battered badly. Jack went to his corner at the end of the frame with gore smeared over his face. But it was no different with Anderson.

For four rounds the bout was a humdinger, an awesome give-and-take battle, with 12 minutes of tough fighting to please the most critical spectators. Jack was knocked off his pins several times, but quickly jumped back into the battle.

Dempsey, trying to make good in his first New York appearance, was wild. He missed often but when he did land, he shook his opponent. Frequently, Anderson fell into a clinch to stop from going down.

After the whipping Dempsey had received in the early rounds, the crowd wondered what enabled him to go on. He came from behind to win a heavy-hitting battle, according to the newspapermen present. Officially it was a no-decision contest.

McArdle wasted no time in signing Dempsey to another contract for a ten-round bout; this time with a swinging, two-fisted slugger named Wild Bert Kenny.

"All I want is to make good in New York," said Dempsey to Gibson and McArdle.

"I don't care who you pick for my opponent."

Billy and Tom liked that kind of talk. They told Dempsey that if he remained in New York he'd find plenty of work in Gibson's club and elsewhere.

Only two weeks had elapsed after Jack's first triumph in New York when he entered the ring to face Kenny on July 8. Reporters who had predicted Jack's failure in his New York debut, again predicted his downfall against an opponent who had engaged in many bruising battles in New York. But Jack went the full distance of ten rounds in a thrilling affair that ended in a newspaper draw.

In the second round, the fans were treated to furious combat, each of the contestants tossing punches from all angles.

In that round Bert received a vicious right to the jaw that almost ended the affair. The bell clanged while Bert was holding the ropes. That alone saved him from dropping to the canvas.

In the fourth round another explosive right, the bell again coming to Kenny's rescue.

The final round was a classic in violence. The pair stood near the ropes and fired away at each other, while covered with gore that flowed freely from nose and mouth. The spectators were cheering madly as the bout neared its finish.

Short hooks to the body put Kenny down three times in that session, but he was saved again by the gong.

A novice fighting an experienced pugilist, Manassa Jack didn't know how to follow up his advantage in punishing power.

It was a great finish for Dempsey. He was a hit with fans and promoter. When Dempsey left the ring, he received a warm ovation.

Six days later, on July 14, Jack appeared at the Harlem Sporting Club to fight John Lester Johnson. That was the fight that soured Dempsey on New York City.

After his Kenny fight, Jack was promised a purse of $500 if he agreed to fight Johnson. Dempsey had received but $45 for his second New York bout, so the guarantee of $500 for the Johnson contest looked good to Jack and he quickly accepted the offer. However, when the battle had been completed, he received only $100, because of the machinations of John the Barber.

Dempsey protested vigorously, but in vain. There was no protection from a boxing commission at that time. Such treatment could not happen today.

Jack scaled 171 for that bout. He looked like a pygmy stacked up against this burly African with a power reputation. One of Dempsey's ribs was broken in the second round. Despite that handicap, Jack carried on to the final bell.

He had been impressive, staggering his opponent often. And now the critics' attitude toward Dempsey changed. They praised this young Westerner and predicted a bright future for him. At last Dempsey had gained the Gotham accolade.

Shortly after this bout with Johnson, Dempsey married the first of his four wives—Maxine Cates, of Walla Walla, Washington. Jack was only 21, Maxine 36. At one time, Maxine had played piano in a Salt Lake City saloon.

Maxine was later used by the government as a witness in Jack's draft-evasion case, in which Dempsey was found innocent of all charges. However, Maxine's testimony proved very damaging to Manassa Jack's case in particular and to his career in general.

Dempsey and Maxine were divorced after two years of marriage. The divorce was granted shortly before Jack stopped Fred Fulton in one round in July 1918.

6

JACK WAS DELIGHTED with the reports in New York newspapers, but he was bitter over being cheated. He decided to invade another area and left with his brother for Philadelphia, where, he was informed, he would be in a more friendly atmosphere. But things didn't turn out that way. There was no work for him. He returned to the West in the early fall of 1916.

In Salida, Colorado, he knocked out Young Hector in the third round. In Ely, Nevada, he beat Terry Keller in ten, and in Salt Lake City he defeated Dick Gilbert in ten. Those were contests in his 1916 campaign that raised him to public consideration. But he still had a long way to go.

And he still required a lively, dependable manager. He had fired, with no reluctance, Reisler; he didn't approve of the work of his brother Bernie; so now he was on his own.

There have appeared many stories on how he and Jack Kearns became associated, the majority of which are hokum. The yarn most often spun is that the Manassa Mauler was in a saloon fight in Oakland in which he floored his assailants.

Kearns arrived on the scene. After leaving the saloon with Dempsey, Kearns induced the fighter to come under his management.

Dempsey denies the occurrence. This is how he explains his association with Kearns:

"I was in Salt Lake City in mid-1917 when I received a letter from Kearns, who was in San Francisco on business. A fighter named Joe Bond had been under Kearns' management when I defeated him in 1916. Kearns, in his note, asked me to join him. He was living in Oakland then.

"I had fought two draws with Al Norton, and had knocked him out in a third bout. I had also won from Willie Meehan in a four-round contest. Kearns figured I was a good prospect. He wrote and asked if I would like to have him manage me.

"I had heard a lot about Kearns and figured he'd be a big help. With his letter, he enclosed a five-dollar bill and a railroad ticket from Salt Lake City to Oakland. I quickly accepted.

"I sent word to Kearns and was informed by him that he had arranged for me to fight Meehan in San Francisco. Five days after my arrival, I fought him. Willie was a popular fighter and drew well in California. Three thousand fans turned out for the fight.

"I was nervous and didn't show my true fighting form. The change of management apparently had affected me. The bout ended in a draw. It was an interesting affair, a crowd-pleasing contest.

"This was my first fight under the management of Kearns. When he returned from San Francisco, he brought me to his home in Oakland, where I lived for a while. Mrs. Kearns, a kindly person, took good care of me. She treated me like a son. That's the true story of my first association with Kearns as my manager."

Kearns, one of eleven managers in Dempsey's checkered career, guided the fighter from his rough stages through the major contests while promoter Tex Rickard's skills brought millions into the coffers of the pair. Dempsey, Kearns, and Rickard made up the first spectacular moneymaking combine in ring history.

Kearns, a master ballyhoo artist, did a wonderful job in bringing Dempsey into the spotlight. His shrewdness obtained for Manassa Jack the title shot with Willard. And it was Kearns' managerial genius that turned the fighter into a national figure and a millionaire.

Rickard was also a master, but in the promotional field. He was a gambler with a flair for the boxing business. Tex made boxing a big business but he couldn't have accomplished it without Dempsey's prowess and Kearns' managerial touch.

In 1925, the twilight of Dempsey's career, the two Jacks had a tiff and their long friendship came to an end. It was brought to a head by Kearns' objection to Dempsey's marriage to Estelle Taylor. Dempsey strongly resented Kearns' interference. Many attribute Dempsey's loss of the championship to Gene Tunney in Philadelphia, the following year, to legal harassment suffered by Manassa Jack while training for the fight.

In reviewing his break with Kearns, Dempsey remarked:

"I liked Jack. He did a lot for me while I was heading toward the top, but he also did a lot of things which I regarded as not so good, though not done intentionally, I would add.

"Kearns was a man with brilliant ideas, originality, and initiative, but he was thoughtless. I met him for the first time in 1917 after he had offered to manage me. He was very sharp, a good manager, shrewd, but sometimes carried things too far in handling me.

"He always had me in good fighting condition; but he really didn't have to worry about me. I was always in fighting trim. Our break was unfortunate, but it had to come because of conditions he brought about."

When in 1950 Dempsey and Kearns were dinner guests at a sports gathering in New York's Hotel Edison, on which occasion Manassa Jack received the much esteemed Fighter of the Half-Century Award, Dempsey went out of his way to give Kearns full credit for his part in leading him up the ladder to fistic fame.

The death of Jack Kearns in 1963 brought forth many stories about his break with Dempsey, some of which Manassa Jack objected to. In a few obituaries, Kearns was depicted not only as the "mastermind" but as one without whom Dempsey would not have fared well financially in his rise to boxing renown. Dempsey, while appreciative of Kearns' role in his fight career, resented the supposition that he could not have reached the heights without the handling of Kearns. Other obituaries overlooked many leading elements in Dempsey's break with Kearns. I queried Manassa Jack about one particular story concerning his break with Kearns.

"I fought Firpo when I was broke," related Dempsey. "My share came to $509,000. My purse for the Willard fight was $27,500. For the bout with Miske, I received $55,000. My purse for the fight with Bill Brennan was $100,000, and the amount for the fight with Tom Gibbons at Shelby [Montana] was $250,000. In all, it ran to nearly a million dollars, yet I had nothing to show for it, at least nothing of a substantial nature—no real money, considering the large amounts involved.

"The answer? Jack Kearns. He spent money like a crazy man. He would go into a nightclub, give $1,000 to a bartender, $2,000 to some girl he fancied, or perhaps toss $5,000 on a table for a grab fest. It was fantastic—plumb crazy!

"I never was too bright with money. But I had seen days when I was eating handouts, and I had known tough times, hungry times, and I was beginning to get frightened. I feared that all the money I had obtained had slipped through my hands and that I would end up just like I began in the fight game—a bouncer, a hobo.

"So I went to see Tex Rickard. He was a great fellow and my good friend. I told him my situation. I had no contract with Kearns and told Rickard so.

"I informed Tex that Jack owed me $300,000 and that I was broke. I also told him I wanted my money for the Firpo fight in advance. I didn't want anyone else drawing on it.

"Rickard agreed. He gave me the money. I put $200,000 in a trust fund for myself at four percent interest. The other $100,000 I placed in a bank.

"The day after the fight, Kearns phoned. He wanted to know what had happened. I told him I had the money and what I had done.

" 'You're crazy,' he said. 'I could have gotten you twenty percent.'

"I had the $300,000 he owed me in the bank. I could have given him nothing, but I guess I parted with $100,000 to him, and I'm sure he got rid of that pretty fast. He was one of the big all-time spenders.

"Our relationship went from bad to worse. Finally, in 1925, we had a showdown. I told him I no longer wanted him as my manager, but that in view of our past affiliation, I was willing to give him 33 percent of my earnings instead of the 50 percent he had been getting. He said it must be 50 or nothing, so I told him I had heard him for the last time, and that's the way we parted.

"I made money out of the Tunney and Sharkey fights. I made myself independent. The story of Kearns' having piloted me to the heavyweight throne is a little overdone. I picked up pointers from Jim Corbett, a grand fellow; Jim Jeffries, who helped teach me his own left-hook technique; Kid McCoy, who taught me the corkscrew blow; and a lot of other great fighters of a day when fighting was a far greater science than it is now.

"Kearns was a great ballyhoo artist and got lots of publicity for me. That, as you know, is very important for one who is trying to advance as a championship contender. Kearns and I were chummy and acted more like brothers than manager and meal ticket. The fact that we didn't have a contract was sufficient evidence of our mutual friendship prior to our breakup. He got good matches for me where other managers might have found it a difficult task. But the fact that I was able to hold my own and come through with victories undoubtedly kept our alliance closely knitted.

"After he and I had joined in partnership, my rise in the fight world definitely got under way. A fight I lost before he became my manager was with Jim Flynn in Murray, Utah, February 13, 1917. That's when the bout was halted in the opening round.

"I've heard it said that I went into the tank for that fight, but it's not true. What happened was that Flynn hit me a power punch that shook me up. I didn't have any real pro handler in my corner. My brother was taking care of me again, and as is usual in such cases, he thought I was badly hurt, got scared, and tossed the towel into the ring.

"That's the true story. I could have continued if he had not interfered.

"A year later I fought Flynn again and knocked him out in the first round."

The question as to whether Dempsey or Kearns was responsible for Manassa Jack's rise to fame may never be answered definitively.

But I doubt that Dempsey would have landed as high in his profession as he did without the able assistance of Kearns. Kearns was one who knew the ropes in boxing as few others did. It was Kearns' persistence in pushing his fighter into the headlines that played the biggest part in the climb of Dempsey to the heights.

Dempsey as he looked in early 1919, before meeting and slaughtering Jess Willard at Toledo.

Willard, conqueror of Jack Johnson at Havana in 1915, shows us his stuff.

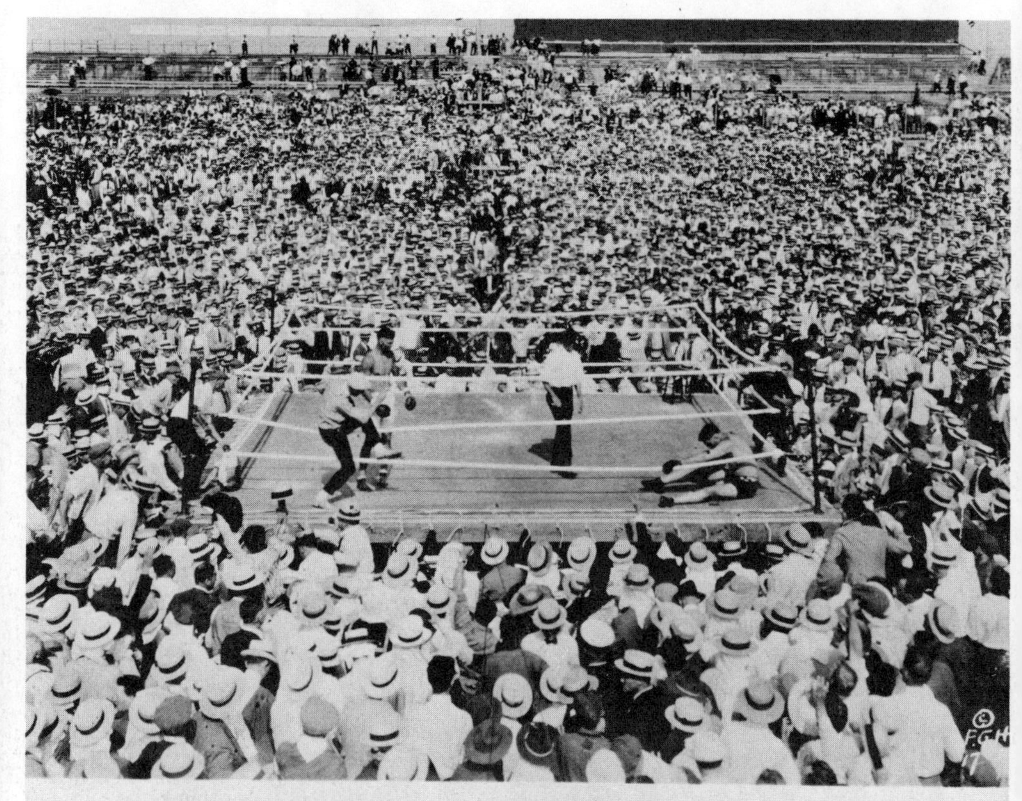

DEMPSEY-WILLARD, TOLEDO, JULY 4, 1919

Big Jess, sitting helplessly on the canvas at the end of the first round, is eyed by Dempsey, Jack Kearns (climbing into the ring), and Referee Ollie Pecord. It appeared to be a KO for Jack, but timekeeper said bell was rung in error. So contest resumed, with Willard unable to answer the bell for the fourth round.

Dempsey (in tux) surrounded by clowns during a vaudeville appearance at the Hippodrome in New York in 1920.

Dempsey the hunter, astraddle his trusty steed, going after bear, deer, and wildcat in the early 1920s.

Bill Brennan (dark trunks) and Dempsey square off prior to their bout in New York's Madison Square Garden on December 14, 1920. Others, from left, are Leo P. Flynn (Brennan's manager), Referee Billy Haukop, Jack Kearns, and ring announcer Joe Humphreys.

A portrait of the Manassa Mauler in 1920.

Kearns and Dempsey shortly after arriving in New York, and just before the Carpentier bout, in which they find their pot of gold.

7

FEW WHO FOLLOW BOXING are aware that Jack Dempsey was as good a hunter as he was a pugilist. Marty Burke, a heavyweight of ability who often worked with Jack, related an experience that Dempsey and he had in 1924 with a grizzly bear, an experience in which Marty's life was threatened. It was saved, according to Burke, by a perfect shot from Dempsey's rifle.

"We were on a short hunting trip in the hills of New Mexico," said Marty, "when deep in a snowdrift we found ourselves confronted by a bear. He came in charging me. I yelled to Jack. With rifle resting in the snow, Dempsey quickly pulled it to his shoulder, aimed, and fired. The shot hit the bear between the eyes, killing him instantly. I've been out on many hunting trips and believe me, I never saw a more perfect kill than that.

"If ever courage was tested, that encounter with the bear did it. That animal was prepared to tear me apart. It took a hell of a lot of courage for Jack to halt that beast in its tracks.

"Talk about a cool, fearless hunter! Jack was one that day!

"Once," continued Marty, "on a trip into the Canadian wilds, one of our dogs was badly wounded. Part of his body was ripped. Jack got off his horse, petted the dog for a few minutes, then remarked:

" 'I better put him out of his misery.'

"He then shot the animal.

"By now the snow had turned into a blizzard. It was one of the worst storms I've ever been through. The roads were impassable, but Dempsey and our guide led the way toward our camp. On the road our dogs were attacked by several foxes before a few shots sent them scattering up the hills.

"When we approached the camp, we discovered two deer, one of which Jack killed with the first shot.

"On another occasion, a wounded moose almost put an end to Dempsey's career. We were accompanied on that hunt by Bob Edgren of the *New York World;* Walter Hinds, of Portland, Maine, one of Jack's friends; Al Currier, Jr.; Dr. Pierce; Jerry Luvadis, who trained Jack; and Dempsey's brother, Joe.

"We went into the woods near Havelock, New Brunswick, between Saint John and Moncton, along the Kennebecasis River, and broke into small groups to hunt for deer. It wasn't long before Dempsey spied some moose tracks.

He had been practicing the moose call and figured he would get the animal in closer range, but his plan didn't work. The moose didn't appear. Jack was keenly disappointed and we decided to stay another day to please him.

"On that final day Jack again spied moose tracks, but his desire to bag the animal in a hurry shooed the creature off. Edgren, an excellent shot, was standing nearby. He blocked the passage of the huge animal.

"The beast turned in Dempsey's direction. Jack never moved. He stood with rifle aimed and fired three shots, each of which hit the moose, who by now was a wild creature.

"Maddened by pain, the animal headed for Dempsey. Jack, thinking his shots had put the enraged creature out for good, had dropped his gun. As the infuriated animal leaped forward, Jack quickly grabbed his rifle and blasted away. He struck the moose in the head and made the kill. Had he missed, he never would have seen the dawn of another day. We marveled at the accuracy of his shots."

Yet another experience on that hunting trip was recalled by

Marty. It was an adventure with a mountain lion and a bobcat.

"Each was snarling, teeth showing, body primed for the leap. It seemed the only person in our group set for the attack was Dempsey. All he required to put the cat away was one shot. He let go and the bullet struck the animal above the eyes. A perfect shot.

"He did the same with the mountain lion, but it took more than the first shot. The animal made a flying leap when the first shot struck home, but like a flash, Jack put a second bullet through the lion's head for the kill.

"Few in the boxing world knew of Dempsey's rating as a hunter. His closest friends who accompanied him on hunting trips, however, recognized his skill. He was, above all, unafraid.

"On another occasion we were on a hunting expedition in which the party consisted of eight men. We were returning from an overnight trip, working our way through a snowstorm, when a big bear spotted us. He came charging in.

"We weren't prepared for that, since we had seen no tracks. I was about to pull the trigger when Dempsey shouted, 'Don't shoot! Don't shoot! Leave him to me!'

"I stepped aside to take shelter. Our four dogs kept circling the bear, who attacked one of the dogs, badly injuring it.

"Dempsey drove his horse near the grizzly, aimed his weapon, pulled the trigger, and the animal dropped dead. One shot was sufficient. I never saw a hunter with more skill. One felt very safe with him in the party on a hunting trip."

Recently I asked if he thought he had retained his shooting eye. Dempsey replied:

"You've got to keep at it if you expect to hold your skill. I enjoyed hunting trips, but business before pleasure, you know.

"I haven't done much in that line since the death of my pal, Max Waxman. There's a lot of business that requires my attention, so the pleasure of hunting is something I can experience only occasionally. I miss the outdoor life to which I was accustomed when I was an active boxer."

In many respects, Dempsey followed in the footsteps of Jim Jeffries, who, by those who knew him best, was listed as the best hunter of wild game among boxers.

Dempsey was in Kentucky training in the early 1920s. One morning he decided to go on a fishing trip. Accompanied by a young guide and one of the local reporters, he started up the mountain on a long, winding path to reach a swift-running stream. About a mile up, they were startled by the appearance of a grim-looking mountaineer who had his rifle pointed at the group. He ordered the invaders to explain their trespassing. Apparently the man thought Dempsey and his companions were federal agents looking for stills.

"I'm Jack Dempsey," said Jack, "and these are my friends. We're out to do a little fishing. I am the heavyweight champion."

"Dempsey? The 'eavyweight champeen? What's all this got to do with yer bein' 'ere?" grunted the mountaineer, shooting tobacco juice over Jack's shoulder. "What's a 'eavyweight champeen?"

Dempsey attempted to explain but didn't get far. The doubter with the rifle was not interested.

"So yure a fistfighter," he exclaimed as he tossed another load of tobacco essence.

The rifleman came closer, took a good look at Dempsey and his comrades, and with a sneer remarked:

"We got plenty like yer 'ere. So yure a fighter, eh? Why any of my kids kin whup yer. Git goin'. And swift, too. We don need yer roun' us. This ain't no place fer a bunch o' snoopin' Yankees that comes 'ere to spy on us."

Dempsey laughed and tried to straighten things out, but without success. The old geezer poked his Winchester into Jack's ribs. Dempsey and his pals quickly started down the trail.

"Never foller a mountain stream up this way. 'Member that," the local admonished. "It ain't 'ealthy."

Dempsey and company went back to the hotel where the newsmen got a good laugh out of the tale. But a pretty waitress, taking in the story of woe, laughed more loudly than the reporters, as she remarked:

"Funny, that's my daddy. He ain't never 'eard of Jack Dempsey, 'cause he cain't read nor write. He's awatchin' fer rev'nu snoopers, the troublemakers fer us. You know, them Yankee agents."

8

A TURNING POINT in Dempsey's rise to becoming a serious heavyweight challenger came in his battle with Gunboat Smith in San Francisco, October 2, 1917. Smith was a pile-driving, walloping heavyweight, as tough an opponent as Kearns could have selected to test the fighting qualities of Dempsey. The contest was staged in San Francisco and drew a sellout gathering.

The Gunner was at the height of his career. He was a dangerous hitter. The affair proved to manager Kearns what he was eager to learn—that Manassa Jack possessed a fighting heart, that he could take a heavy wallop without withering.

In telling the story of that power-punching affair, Dempsey said that it was one of the three toughest battles he had fought in the early days of his career.

"I had heard plenty about the Gunner's socking power, his deadly occipital punch, and his gameness. The occipital blow was one around the neck which, when delivered with full force, was likely to batter the recipient into a state of numbness.

"I won the opening round, according to the newspapers, because I didn't give the Gunner an opportunity to throw his right, his power blow. But it was different in the second round.

"I had lowered my guard and, like a flash, the Gunner whipped over his right. The punch landed with terrific force on my jaw. It came in a sweeping movement and it struck with sledge-hammer power. My knees sagged and Kearns, standing on a stool outside my corner, fell and was momentarily dazed.

"After the fight, Kearns said he thought that I had suffered heavy injury. The punch, he declared, carried power, and he figured I had been knocked out. Instead, there I was in a stupor, out on my feet and fighting back as if nothing had happened."

Here Jack turned over a clipping, containing a report of the bout. "Read the rest of the story, Nat," he said. "Here it is":

"When Jack got back to his corner for the minute's rest, his seconds worked feverishly over him. He sat like one who was doped.

"Dempsey's seconds pushed him out of his corner when the gong sounded for the third round, and Kearns, who by now had expected to see his fighter knocked out, instead saw him go all out, taking the Gunner's best shots and delivering many good ones in return.

"In the fourth and final round, he fought like a maniac. When the gong sounded ending the fight, Referee Toby Irwin raised the hand of Dempsey, the winner.

"Most of the spectators agreed with the decision and gave Dempsey rounds of applause. But they wondered how Jack had survived the punishment he had received in the second round."

Gunboat Smith was very angry at the verdict. Asked by the sports editor of the *Examiner* what he thought, Smith replied:

"No one except Dempsey could have gone on after the punishment I handed to him. I thought I had him in the second round. I think I should at least have received a draw."

When Dempsey regained his senses, he sheepishly remarked to Kearns:

"Doc, I'm sorry. I have plenty to learn. I lost, didn't I?"

"Lost, you fool! You won. The referee gave you the decision."

"What are you saying, Doc? You're kiddin'."

A few years after the fight, Frank Herman, former sports

editor of the *San Francisco Bulletin,* visited me. During our talk on boxing he remarked:

"Dempsey proved he had the necessary ammunition stowed away in his gloves to smash his way to victory when he won that match with Gunboat Smith. The Gunner was a terrific puncher, one who could battle as Jack did. If Jack had lost that contest, I think he never would have won the world crown. That bout, in my opinion, was the turning point in his career."

A few weeks after that fight Dempsey faced Carl Morris, the Tulsa, Oklahoma, giant who weighed 235 pounds to Jack's 185. Morris had a 9½-inch reach advantage, 81 to 71½. That fight took place November 2, 1917, in San Francisco, and Dempsey carried off the honors. It was a four-round event in which Jack outmaneuvered, outgeneraled, outpointed, and outfought his opponent.

In the victories over Smith and Morris, Dempsey came through his tests with flying colors. Those two battles were turning points in his rise to a title bout with Willard.

Kearns gave Morris another chance at Jack in a return contest at Buffalo, New York, on February 4, 1918. In that encounter, Manassa Jack climbed a step higher by handing the Sapulpa Giant an unmerciful beating, winning on a foul in the sixth round. Carl was battered all over the ring.

From the second round to the finish, Dempsey forced the issue. In the fourth session, Morris's nose was bleeding badly and he started to lose confidence. The referee warned Morris in the following session, when his punches were low.

That continued through the sixth round, in which frame Morris was unsteady and confused. He lifted a right almost from the floor and struck Dempsey low. The referee shooed him to his corner and awarded the fight to Dempsey.

Thus Morris's attempt to gain top place as the leading contender for Willard's crown came to naught, while that of Dempsey gained impetus. Jack had climbed another notch.

Later the same year Dempsey faced Morris for a third time. In the Louisiana Auditorium in New Orleans, Jack stopped Carl with his first punch, after a little maneuvering. It was a left hook to the solar plexus. The punch immediately dropped Morris and Referee Remy Dorr counted him out as he lay unconscious.

At the clang of the bell, Morris had rushed forth and forced Dempsey against the ropes. Jack blocked, twisted out of a clinch, then brought up a half hook, half uppercut with his left that ended the affair.

After the bout was over, Morris was asked by a reporter how he felt.

"I thought a ton of bricks struck me," replied Carl. "That was some punch. It paralyzed me."

Bill Brennan was another fighter Kearns was eager to have Dempsey eliminate. Brennan was a top heavyweight with a good record. He was managed by the loquacious Leo P. Flynn. Kearns figured that if Manassa Jack could whip Brennan, another huge step forward would have been taken. Brennan, in a moment of underestimation, believed that Manassa Jack wasn't ready to tackle him and thus regarded the match as a breather.

He was sadly mistaken. Brennan was knocked out by Dempsey in the sixth round by a blow struck with such force that it fractured Bill's ankle when he landed on his back. Brennan was dropped four times in the second round. He was saved from a knockout by the bell.

Thus, over a stretch of one month, Dempsey had put away Homer Smith and Jim Flynn, each in the first round, Brennan in six, and had whipped Carl Morris.

While Dempsey was methodically making headway toward national recognition, Kearns was continuing the ballyhoo campaign in his fighter's behalf. Nothing that would advertise was overlooked. Introductions at functions, greeting sports folk in prestige places like Chicago's Morrison Hotel, issuing a steady stream of reports on Dempsey's prowess and progress to the national press, showcasing his fighter's workouts, especially in those gymnasiums where it was known that leading sportsmen hung out—these were but a few of the efforts of Kearns in his buildup of Dempsey, a buildup that very few other fighters were able to obtain.

The talkative manager blew the flame where it did the most good. He knew the big shots, the sports "tops," and he could make them listen attentively as he boosted the stock of

Manassa Jack, "the next champion of the world." And Kearns could get positive results.

Though not always. There were some skeptics, but not too many. When later, in the summer of 1918, the two Jacks would head east in quest of a fight with Fred Fulton, a few newspapers would still not be as enthusiastic about Dempsey as Kearns would have liked them to be. The swing east would be crucial. Kearns knew it. He could not now, in preparing for that trip, afford any loss of prestige for Dempsey.

For the six-foot, five-and-one-half-inch Fred Fulton was one fighter who could guarantee Dempsey a good press, that is, if Manassa Jack could take him. But more, Kearns regarded Fulton as the front runner who stood tallest in Dempsey's path to a championship bout. Beating Fulton would assure a title shot. But in order to do battle with Fulton, skirmishes awaited both Jacks. Dempsey's came first and proved easier—seven early-round knockouts plus a no-decision contest. Among those kayoed was Fred Saddy—a first-round victim—who after his retirement from the ring became the boxing commissioner of Wisconsin. Only the no-decision contest, with Billy Miske on May 3, gave Manassa Jack a good workout.

Kearns' skirmishes were yet to come.

9

Doc Kearns went all out to change the habits of Dempsey once the road to fame approached. New clothes, stopping in big cities where the publicity he sought for his fighter would be of a higher caliber than that in the smaller locales, checking in at expensive hotels, eating in top restaurants—all these brought a new life to and better publicity for the boxer Kearns was aiming to take to the top. Perhaps most symbolic of this new life was Dempsey's new mode of travel—in Pullman drawing rooms, a severe contrast to Jack's rod-riding days. Travel Pullman-style proved an effective morale booster, and also bound tighter the ties of friendship between manager and fighter.

It was quite a change from the poverty Jack had experienced during his earlier boxing days, days still firmly imprinted on his memory. With Kearns' aid, Dempsey was making the climb but it was a tough haul, as both pilot and boxer came to realize.

But Kearns had sharp eyes. He knew all the tricks of the trade, was thoroughly acquainted with the caliber of the talent Dempsey would have to shunt to the sidelines, and went about the job of selling his pugilist by setting up his own elimination series.

He searched through the list of eligibles for a title match and decided to have Manassa Jack eliminate them one by one. One top heavyweight after another, each a claimant for a title shot with Willard, was matched with Dempsey. None survived the test. Thus Manassa Jack continued his successful rise as challenger.

Kearns was ever the master tactician. Once he decided on plans to get his fighter to the top, there was no stopping him. He had been working his meal ticket at an incredible pace. But the fast pace was only part of his scheme. Kearns' eye was on a trip to New York, but the timing had to be right. In New York things usually happened, and he had to be really sure his fighter would be equal to what he hoped would happen.

Now the time was ripe. So off to New York went Kearns. With Kearns sniffing a title shot, he knew whom he'd have to see, and work on—Tex Rickard.

Kearns' friend, John McGraw, manager of the New York Giants baseball team, introduced him to Rickard in the Biltmore Hotel. Jack immediately began booming the stock of Dempsey, but Rickard was not impressed.

"He's the next heavyweight champion of the world, Mr. Rickard," vociferated Kearns. "I'm seeking a match for him with Willard."

"He's too small," replied Tex.

"That's what you said when I discussed Les Darcy with you," retorted Kearns.

"What do you know about Darcy?" asked Rickard.

"Plenty," returned Kearns. "I induced Darcy to make the trip to New York and you tried to steal him," charged Kearns.

Rickard was angry. Pointing his finger at Kearns, he asked, "Haven't I seen you before?"

"You certainly have," replied Kearns; "at your joint in Alaska. Why don't you put on a Dempsey-Willard fight? It's the best match in the field today. Why are you hesitating?"

"Dempsey is too small. He's no match for Jess. Do you want a killing on your hands? The public won't stand for such a match. They'll approve a Fulton-Willard bout far more readily than a Willard-Dempsey contest. Your man doesn't fit into the picture."

The conversation went on for some time along the same lines until Kearns, urged by McGraw, offered to put Dempsey against Fulton in an elimination bout. Of course, a bout with Fulton secretly pleased horsetrader Kearns.

"If Fulton's manager agrees, I'll make the match," snapped Kearns to Tex. "If Jack wins, I'll expect you to give him a crack at the title."

Then softening his tone, Kearns continued, "You can do it, Tex. You're a master promoter. You can make plenty of dough on a fight between my Jack and Big Jess."

But Rickard was adamant. As things then stood, he couldn't see Dempsey as an opponent for Jess.

There hadn't been a heavyweight championship fight in the United States in over two years and boxing followers were anxious for one. So Kearns' publicity campaign for his fighter received more than sympathetic attention.

Kearns did get the Fulton match, and Dempsey went to Long Branch, New Jersey, to train for it. There he was under the expert supervision of veteran Jimmy DeForest and his aides, Battling Johnson and the Jamaica Kid.

DeForest's eagle eyes were focused on Dempsey's every move. He was an excellent teacher. His task, however, was made easier by the fact that Manassa Jack was in superb physical condition, thanks to the many recent bouts arranged by Kearns.

As Kearns had foreseen, Dempsey's victory over Fulton was to be *the* turning point in Manassa Jack's rise to the position of number-one contender for Willard's crown. But even the prescient Kearns must have been delightfully shocked at the outcome of the Fulton contest.

On July 27, 1918, at the old Federal League ballpark in Harrison, New Jersey, Dempsey, now 23, knocked out the 27-year-old Fulton in the first round. Scarce had the opening bell rung than Fulton found his cause doomed. Dempsey, at 188 pounds, 20 lighter than his foe, let go a crunching left hook to the stomach that found its target. Fred doubled up, but his chin was left free, inviting Jack's right. Dempsey obliged, smashing it against Fulton's jaw. The fight was over. The time, 18 3/5 seconds.

After that power display against a much larger opponent, there was no stopping Kearns in his pursuit of Willard. He kept Dempsey in fighting trim by pitting him against top heavyweights and second-raters. Terry Keller, Jack Moran, Battling Levinsky, Porky Flynn, Carl Morris, Gunboat Smith all fell via the kayo. He fought another no-decision with Billy Miske, this time a six-rounder. Before the Miske bout, Jack had dropped a four-round decision to Fat Willie Meehan in San Francisco, September 13, 1918. It was to be Manassa Jack's last loss until 1926, the first Tunney fight.

In five contests, all in the early part of 1919, from January through April, Dempsey shunted all his opponents to the sidelines via the knockout route, each in the first round.

Dempsey now had completed his apprenticeship. He had faced every heavyweight the public figured was entitled to a match. One by one, with the exception of Willie Meehan, he left them by the wayside, either by knockout or by decision.

Now Kearns was positive that Rickard could not turn down a bout with Willard. No longer was Tex's excuse that Dempsey was too light and too small to face Willard fistically logical.

There were still many who thought that Manassa Jack was not yet a suitable opponent, but Kearns' arguments were so strong and convincing that he finally gained Rickard's support. Ever since Dempsey's dramatic kayo of Fulton, Tex had looked upon the Manassa Mauler in a different light.

Tex told Kearns to send a message to Willard asking if he would fight Dempsey.

"Glad to oblige if Rickard consents," Jess answered.

That was all Kearns required—Willard's willingness to have Dempsey as his opponent.

Rickard asked Kearns how much he wanted for Dempsey's services.

"We should get $30,000 to cover expenses, plus our fee for the fight," Jack replied.

That angered Tex. "Let's call it off," snapped Rickard as he started for the door.

At this point two men entered the room. They were Cubans, stooges for Kearns. He had arranged to have them make a fabulous offer to buy out Rickard so that they could stage the fight in Havana. Rickard was not aware of the plot.

"Wait, Tex," said Kearns as Rickard was walking toward the door. "I've brought these two men here. They represent a syndicate and will buy you out for $200,000."

Rickard hit the floor with his cane as he ordered the men to leave. Then turning to Kearns, he shouted:

"I want the match but expect you to get down to earth. Lower your demands. I want to make a little profit, not take a heavy loss."

They walked back to renew the negotiations. Kearns had pulled a master stroke. The Cubans were waiters paid by Kearns.

Rickard and Kearns devised a plan to settle their money differences. Turning to Bob Edgren, sports editor of the *New York World,* who was at the conference, Kearns suggested that reporters in an adjoining room should be assembled, told of the differences, and permitted to help settle the problem.

When the writers were informed by Kearns and Edgren of the plan, they cast secret ballots that organized the heavyweight championship bout. Kearns had won for Dempsey. Kearns had scored heavily in a battle of wits with the man who was molding the period that would go into history as the greatest since the inauguration of glove matches—the Golden Era of Boxing.

Had Kearns not been so insistent, had he not pushed his plan, Dempsey would not have obtained the title match. Having gotten Rickard's okay, the bout was now assured.

With the announcement that a Dempsey-Willard bout was definite, there came considerable criticism from recognized experts who figured that Jess was too big and too strong for Jack. Former champions Jack Johnson and Jim Jeffries were among those who didn't think a wise match had been hatched.

Following a conference with Kearns in Rickard's office, Tex, Kearns, and Ike Dorgan, Rickard's publicity director, boarded a ferry for New Jersey, where Rickard decided officially to sign Dempsey for the Willard contest.

There wasn't much about Big Jess to grip public imagination other than his six feet six inches and the fact that he had brought back to the Caucasians the world heavyweight title from Jack Johnson in 1915.

For some months Rickard had been on the hunt for an opponent for the Pottawatomie Giant, one who could arouse public excitement. Now he had him—or so Jack Kearns had convinced the promoter. But Rickard still wasn't one hundred percent convinced, even after the signing, that Manassa Jack was the most suitable foe from the point of view of the gate. But whenever he raised a doubt or two, the persuasive Kearns seemed always to be able to pacify Tex.

Professional pugilism was taboo in many parts of the United States. So even though the agreement had been reached in a New York hotel, it was necessary for Tex to go over to New Jersey to have the articles signed. It was also Rickard's aim to avoid Jack Curley, who had an agreement with Kearns, and John (the Barber) Reisler, each of whom was trying to get a stranglehold on the match. Reisler and Curley claimed prior rights to Jack's services.

After the signing ceremonies in Weehawken, New Jersey, a smiling Willard, his guarantee assured by Rickard, remarked:

"I want immunity against any injury suffered by Dempsey. Bull Young met accidental death in a battle with me and I don't want a recurrence."

As matters turned out in Toledo, the battle ended with Willard, not Dempsey, in jeopardy.

Jess's remark didn't upset Dempsey. He was aware of the Kansan's strength, powerful frame, and ability, and paid no attention to Willard's warning. Dempsey was also aware of what he himself could do.

Since the matter of Dempsey's guarantee had been settled—the sum of $27,500 was agreed upon—no further hitch was encountered. Willard was to receive $100,000.

Jack Johnson declared that Willard's height and weight advantage would be too great for Dempsey to overcome.

Jim Jeffries issued a statement declaring it would be better for Dempsey if he waited a couple of years before tackling so big and strong a man as Willard.

But the public paid little attention to those prophets of woe. The top experts gave Dempsey more than a fighting chance because of his condition. Willard, at this point in his career, was still a giant but little else.

Fact is, newspaper experts were writing that Willard was ring-rusty. They declared that because of his appearance in a Wild West circus, he had become fat, muscle-bound, overweight, and was decidedly out of training. His involvement with several movies also kept him from achieving the physical fitness one would expect a world champion to display.

Jess found that life could be beautiful as the heavyweight champ, so who needed a training program and sparmates and running and exercises and . . .

Once Governor James Cox of Ohio had sanctioned the fight for his state, Tex's flair for heavyweights was never more in evidence than in his promotion of this extravaganza. He went all out to spark the spirit of the public and enthusiasm for Manassa Jack.

By nature Rickard was a big gambler. He had sought an opponent for Willard who he figured would have the most support from the public. But something within him said that Dempsey was not the man, he admitted—off the record.

But how wrong Tex turned out to be. For in the sunbaked Bay View Park Arena in Toledo, July 4, 1919, it was mayhem—with Big Jess the victim.

10

WITH THE CONSIDERABLE TALK in Toledo about the poor condition of Willard, and with the rumor that Dempsey had worked like a beaver in preparation for the contest, many gamblers switched their wagers to Jack. Notwithstanding, on the afternoon of July 4, there were few in the amphitheater who agreed with the betting gentry. Once the fight was under way, though, the bettors who switched were quickly vindicated.

Dempsey, now 24 and weighing 191, entered the ring with a sullen look. He wore white trunks, and an angry look. The scowl would intensify once the fight was in progress. Bill Tate, one of his trainers, held an umbrella over Jack's head to protect him from the sun's rays.

Big Jess, age 37 and scaling 245, wore blue—an appropriate color, as it turned out. He was cocky, extremely so. He waved to friends at ringside and acted like one who had a cinch ahead of him.

The contrast between the two fighters was noticeable. One, Dempsey, was tight, the other, Jess, relaxed, as they sat in their respective corners awaiting the call of the referee for instructions.

A dramatic fight? One never to be forgotten?

Yes, the drama in this bout rivaled any heavyweight contest in the twentieth century, with the possible exception of the Dempsey-Firpo affair four years later.

In Dempsey, boxing had a sensational young tiger who owned amazing speed of hands and feet, and a power punch; in Willard, the tallest champion since glove contests made their permanent appearance in 1892.

A temperature ranging from 103 to 110 degrees brought on stifling heat that made the spectators wilt. But they forgot their discomfort within a minute after the action commenced.

Willard, arrogantly confident, and Dempsey, nervous, head down, straining at the leash, awaited the gong. Jack scowled as he listened to the instructions of Referee Ollie Pecord.

After a few weeks of training in the hot sun, Dempsey's skin was a deep brown. He had a mean appearance. His heart was set on victory.

The fight was scheduled for twelve rounds but at no time did Dempsey or Kearns believe it would go the limit. The bets placed by both on a first-round knockout clearly indicated that.

Once the fight got under way, the fans were treated to a whirlwind attack by the challenger. The mahogany-hued Manassa Mauler circled his opponent, then moved into action with catfooted quickness. He poked his left to the head, bobbed and weaved, quickly got out of arm's reach of the champion, then crashed a powerful left to the midsection. That punch nearly doubled Willard. It was the first sign of what was in store for the Kansas giant.

Fighting with the fury of a wounded jungle beast, Dempsey went after his prey. One minute and 58 seconds after the opening, the biggest of all champions was a battered hulk. He was dazed, smashed out of all proportion.

The effect of Dempsey's punches was startling. They landed so fast, with such precision, the eyes could hardly follow the flying fists. At each crunching, crashing clout, Willard's face was changed as if his opponent were a sculptor who was dissatisfied with a portrait in clay and was deliberately obliterating it, feature by feature.

Dempsey's hands were in motion all the time. Willard, though tall and heavy, moved about, charging occasionally, but his punches went for naught due to the agility and defensive tactics of the challenger.

Suddenly, as out of a clear sky, came the blow that struck home and started Big Jess on the road to defeat. It was a crashing left to the chin that brought the giant to the canvas.

Up he came, only to be hurled against the ropes by thunderous battering-ram smashes. Another left and down went Jess.

Groggy? Yes, but he again raised himself, a dazed titleholder, tired and game. Down again he went with a crash. He crawled like a wounded animal with his back half-turned as he worked his way up again.

The challenger showed no mercy. He gave no quarter. He overwhelmed Jess with an hysterical burst of fury that sent him down for the fourth time. Now, with fist cocked, ready for the kill, Dempsey stood over his opponent, snarling, as he did later over Luis Firpo.

Willard had no defense against Dempsey's vicious attack. Jess had plenty of courage, but that alone was not enough. He reeled across the ring while Jack kept pumping rights and lefts to the body. The champion again was felled. His gloved hands held the ropes.

Painfully he dragged himself to a half-erect position. A new series of smashes saw Jess collapse into a sitting position, dazed and helpless. Blood flowed from Jess's nose and mouth. His cheeks were swollen and bleeding. The bones in the right cheek were fractured. Several teeth had been knocked out. His lips were gashed. His right eye was swollen and shut. His left eye was inflamed.

That was the nauseating picture of Willard at the end of the opening round. It was a revolting scene. Many ringside veterans turned their heads and hoped for Jess's retirement, but he was too game to quit.

Never had I seen a fighter take such a shellacking. Dempsey was like a bulldog, never to be shaken off. Even when Jess rallied momentarily in the second and third rounds, Dempsey didn't step back. Pantherlike, he feinted and stepped aside to get an opening. Then in he went, again lashing away.

He was cold, calculating, and sure of the effects of his blows.

He was every inch the fighter, from the squarely set feet to the lowered head and scowling brow.

Dempsey that day fought like a demon. There was no stopping him.

Not in the memory of the oldest fan in that sunbaked arena had anyone seen a fighter take such a beating in a title fight during a single round. In that short period Willard was down seven times!

The gong sounded while Jess was sitting glassy-eyed, his wide-open mouth streaming blood. Pandemonium reigned as his seconds dragged him to his corner after Ollie Pecord had counted him out.

But he wasn't out, despite the fact that Dempsey's hand had been raised in victory and Jack was quietly exiting from the ring.

The referee had been informed by the timekeeper, Warren Barbour, that the gong had sounded at the count of seven and the bout was not over.

Quickly both Kearns and Pecord raced to the ropes and called to Dempsey to return to the ring.

"Come back, Jack! Come back! The fight is not over," Kearns shouted.

Surprises? Yes, indeed! Plenty for that day, and for many another fight day.

The bell clanged, and Willard, somehow, got off his stool to face his tormentor for round two. He jabbed, but the effort was too weak to hurt Jack. Jess proved his courage but no man could continue to take what was dished out by Manassa Jack without losing his strength. Jess's arms and legs were weary, leadlike, yet he carried on—in a doomed cause.

But nothing could check Dempsey. Though there was some slackening of his pace, his attack was still furious. His punches yet accurate and devastating.

While Willard sat in his corner following the termination of the second round, the crowd pleaded for Referee Pecord to end the affair. He ignored the shouting. And Jess went forth for more punishment in the third.

Weak and fatigued, he was a mark for a heavy attack. He was staggered several times, but Jack couldn't put him away. When the gong sounded ending that round, a bloody, battered, half-blinded Willard was virtually dragged to his corner by his handlers. There he motioned to Referee Pecord to approach.

"I cannot continue," he told Pecord. The referee walked over to Dempsey and raised his hand in victory.

A new champion was crowned in a fight I shall never forget. Manassa Jack that day was the greatest human tornado I'd ever seen in the ring. Dempsey's eyes were on one man only. He was the classic gladiator.

From a hobo Dempsey had risen to lay hold of the most valuable crown in boxing. And with that crown, there arrived the Gold Era of Boxing, with its fabulous gates and outstanding matches. It was the beginning of the lush period of ring spectacles—and the million-dollar gate.

Many stories have been written in which Tex Rickard is given the credit for bringing that era into boxing. However, without the assistance of Dempsey and Kearns, Rickard could not have accomplished it.

While training for the Willard fight, Dempsey had a somewhat arcane experience.

Manassa Jack was not a superstitious man, but several of his sparmates were. One in particular was Jim Johnson. He told Jack about a gypsy fortune-teller whose place of business was not far from the camp. Jack, who each day took a long walk, accompanied by trainer Jimmy DeForest, decided to pay her a visit. DeForest relates the incident.

" 'I'm not superstitious,' Jack told me, 'but I'd like to hear what she has to say about the Willard fight.'

" 'I wouldn't do it, Jack,' I replied. 'The fight is only a week off and she may say something that will upset you.'

"No amount of persuasion could change Jack's mind, so I decided to go along with him," continued DeForest. "He was getting restless and I thought the visit would perk him up.

"As a warning note, however, I told Jack it might not be good.

" 'She might upset you,' I said. 'Kearns will then blame me.'

" 'Never mind Kearns,' replied Dempsey. 'We're going.'

"The gypsy was pleasant. She greeted Jack and requested that he seat himself opposite her at a small table.

" 'Are you nervous?' she asked.

" 'No, just curious,' Jack replied.

" 'Got any money with you—silver I mean?'

" 'Yes, a few pieces.'

" 'Well then, we'll get down to business. Place them in my hand,' she commanded, and Jack dropped three silver dollars into her outstretched hand. Looking straight at the champ, she said:

" 'I see two wonderful years for you. They will bring you a fortune. You're going to make a lot of money—not right now, but it won't be long. You'll meet many wealthy people and you'll travel a lot.'

"Then she placed her hands over her eyes, then over Jack's face, and continued talking.

" 'I see some trouble coming to you. You'll have to fight hard to overcome it, but you will. Then you'll become a very rich man. You'll be a very important man. People will bow to you. You'll have many new friends.'

"I never believed in fortune-telling, but that woman changed my mind. Her words struck Jack in the right spot," continued DeForest. "He needed that encouragement to perk him up during that last week of training. Her words acted like magic on him.

" 'Jimmy, I'll win the title and win easily,' remarked Dempsey after the gypsy's prediction.

"The day before the fight Dempsey was as lively as a bird in sunny springtime.

" 'I'll stop him, Jimmy,' Jack joyously remarked as he slapped me on my back. 'What that gypsy predicted is what's going to happen, Jimmy. I'll knock him out in two rounds.'

"Jack was cheerful all of that afternoon. When he weighed in for the fight, he was calm and relaxed. When fight time arrived and he was in his dressing room, he had the usual sour look, was tense, fidgety, but confident that he would win the championship.

"Nat, that's a true story," Jimmy said to me. "You can use it in the *Telegram.* I'm sure Jack will get a kick out of it. I'd never have believed it were I not present. I think a lucky star had brought Jack to that gypsy."

During World War II I was visiting wounded servicemen in a hospital in Denver where they had been brought a few days before from the battlefields of Europe. I related that gypsy yarn as part of my program. The story made a hit.

During the question-and-answer period, one of the wounded lads, sitting in a wheelchair with a charming nurse at his side, got a big laugh when he smilingly remarked:

"Jack won the fight but missed his prediction by one round. How come?"

11

WAS IT A FIRST-ROUND KNOCKOUT?

Many experts at the Toledo ringside thought so, among them Bob Edgren, the original stakeholder, and an international sports figure on the staff of the *New York World.* Edgren, writing his syndicated story, stated emphatically that Dempsey won by a knockout in the opening round. Here is what he wrote:

"Fighting with the fury of a bulldog bearing down on a mastiff, Jack Dempsey knocked out Big Jess Willard in the first round of their heavyweight championship bout in Toledo. But for a series of amazing blunders caused by having amateurs as officials, the bout technically ended at the termination of the third round when Willard called Referee Pecord to his corner to inform him that he could not continue. Ray Archer, Jess's chief second, then tossed in the towel, water-soaked and bloodstained, acknowledging defeat."

When the fight was over and the referee was asked in

what round it terminated, he hesitated, glanced at several ringside reporters, then declared, "It was the third round, since Willard had quit between rounds, during the minute's rest period."

Many writers refused to accept that ruling. They declared that Pecord was hesitant in giving his decision. The majority, however, agreed the bout had ended in the third round since the bell for the fourth had not yet sounded.

Edgren upbraided the officials. He was vehement in his argument that the fight had ended in the first round. Many heavy wagers were lost on Pecord's ruling, both in ordering Dempsey to return to the ring and in deciding on the third round.

To this day the disputes continue whenever a major heavyweight bout comes up for discussion. My opinion is that the decision was correct.

The verdict proved extremely costly to Jack Kearns. He had wagered $10,000 at 10 to 1, that the fight would not go beyond the opening round. Kearns, at my request, visited the *New York Telegram* sports department to discuss that phase of the fight with me. This was his statement:

"Referee Pecord was counting over Jess with right hand bobbing up and down. When he had reached ten, he held up Dempsey's hand to denote the winner. Then the commotion started.

"Jack, in his glee, leaped over the ropes and started on his way to the dressing room. Warren Barbour, the official timer, got up and shouted to Pecord and me that the fight was not over. He said the bell had sounded at the count of seven and saved Jess from a knockout. Pecord and I rushed to the ringside and yelled at Dempsey to return to the ring.

"Dempsey quickly returned, but a minute and 31 seconds had elapsed by this time according to my special timer, Joe Bannon. Then there was another minute's delay before I could get Jack ready. It was a muddle for which I blame Barbour.

"I bet $10,000 of my money and Jack's that Dempsey would score a knockout in the first round. I got 10 to 1 from a bookie friend. I lost the bet fairly. There can be no question about that. Toledo was an open betting town and the wagering was pretty high.

"I was friendly with a betting commissioner, John (Get Rich Quick) Ryan, a smart gambler known all over the country. The liveliest spot in Toledo was the Boody Hotel, the unofficial headquarters. The bookie had rented a ballroom and set up his betting office. About ten days before the fight, I said to him, 'Why don't you open a book on the fight?' He told me he would think about it.

"A few days later, I walked into his headquarters and said, 'Say John, there's a money man who wants to bet on Dempsey winning in the first round. What would the price be against it?'

"He didn't hesitate. 'Ten to one.'

" 'How much does he want to place?' the bookie asked.

" 'About ten grand,' I replied.

" 'Bring him around,' Ryan said.

" 'Oh, no,' I said. 'He doesn't want it known that he's betting. I'll bring the dough over for him.'

"That night, I turned over the $10,000 and the bet was on.

"At the fight, although Warren Barbour was the official timer, I had Joe Bannon, head of the Hearst newspapers delivery department, as my official timer. He was sitting behind Barbour.

"It was difficult to keep count, due to the din and the people standing and yelling, but as Dempsey dropped Jess for the seventh time, Bannon yelled into my ear, 'Ten seconds, Jack.'

"At that moment I knew that I had blown the ten grand. Willard couldn't be counted out in that round.

"But I jumped into the ring at the sound of seven, grabbed Pecord and screeched into his ear, 'He's out! He's out! The fight is finished! Ollie, I've got a new champ! Raise his hand!'

"But Pecord was in a trance. He was all mixed up after what I had shouted. Just as I thought he would follow my instructions, Barbour got Pecord's attention and my move to the referee was lost.

"Meanwhile, Dempsey had gotten out of the ring. I lost my bet fairly," concluded Kearns.

The day after the fight, Willard was interviewed by a reporter from the *Toledo News Bee.* Jess's face was distorted from the smashing he had received, yet he dictated the following:

"I haven't any excuse to offer for my defeat. I was beaten fairly by a better man. Youth was served. In the advantage of weight, reach, and height, I believed I was invincible. I learned my mistake as did Jim Jeffries in the Reno fight.

"Perhaps it would have been better had I trained differently, but I don't think so. The better man won in a hard, fair fight.

"I assume full responsibility for my own training, for the direction of my fight, and for everything connected with it. I had a loyal group around me and the men helped me all they could. I cannot blame anyone in my camp for my defeat.

"A left to the jaw that Dempsey landed in the opening round was the cause of my terrible showing. I was dazed after that and never fully recovered. The loss of blood from my wounded eye affected me. My right eye was almost closed. It bothered me a lot.

"Let no one say that Dempsey lacks the fighting qualities that make for ring greatness. He deserved to win and I congratulate him."

The destruction of Willard was the major feat of Jack Dempsey's fighting career.

With the championship in sight, the goal of his dreams in view, with a new world before him at the age of 24, Dempsey had shown no mercy to the giant facing him.

The explosive power displayed by the Manassa Mauler was beyond belief. The description of the fight is the story of a giant-killer battering his way to the throne by a vicious, relentless attack. Not in the memory of the oldest fan could one recollect when a champion received such severe punishment.

Years later, I inquired of Dempsey about his feelings following his victory over Willard.

"If a man is a pugilist, what greater honor can be achieved than winning the world crown? It's a thrill that lasts long. It meant a lot to me.

"Had I not defeated Jess, I might have quit the ring. My heart was set on the championship and now I had it. Unfortunately the draft situation arose which embittered me and put a sting into my triumph, but when I overcame that and then defeated Carpentier, I was extremely happy for the great change.

"If I remained an ordinary fighter, I would not have had the opportunity to meet the fine people with whom I became friendly after my bout with Carpentier. That fight, I figure, was the real turning point in my career."

"Why the turning point?" I inquired. "Most people figure the winning of the world heavyweight championship to be that mark."

"Well," replied Jack, "the trouble I had in the unfortunate draft case is what I blame for the lukewarm treatment I received for several years, but that was dismissed following my success in the fight with Carpentier. Although it took only ten minutes for the jury to dismiss the case by bringing in a 'Not Guilty' verdict, it took several years for me to obtain the good graces of the public. It was my victory in the Carpentier match that brought it about.

"I cherish that day. It brought me happiness.

"The feeling of being booed prior to the Carpentier success irritated me. I knew I didn't deserve it. It was through my pugilistic power and the quick verdict in my favor by my peers, that the friendly hands of the public were stretched out to greet me as they do to this day. It is an acclaim that gratifies me."

Hanging in my office is a wrinkled righthand boxing glove. On the back of it, stretching almost from the curled fingertip to the wrist, is a dark brown stain. That is a souvenir of the Toledo battle in which Willard was dethroned and Dempsey crowned the new king of the heavyweights.

The blood is that of a brave gladiator who found the terrible beating he had received too much to sustain after three rounds. He could go no further in the vicious battle that cost him the crown.

The man who had been turned down several times when applying for a title shot with Willard was now king of the fighting clan.

12

FOLLOWING HIS VICTORY over Willard, Dempsey, along with Kearns, went on a theatrical tour. The itinerary included many out-of-the-way places. Nothing pleased a rustic more than to tell a friend that he had fought a few rounds with Jack Dempsey.

While on this tour, the two Jacks, following the example of the great John L. Sullivan, decided to offer $1,000 to any person who could last three rounds with Manassa Jack. The Boston Strong Boy had popularized this gimmick and it had served him well. Kearns, born with Madison Avenue instincts, saw no reason why it wouldn't serve his fighter equally well.

The first stop was Trenton, New Jersey. Kearns placed the $1,000 come-on in the local daily paper. On the night of Jack's initial show, Kearns, more than gratified with the ad's success, walked out on the stage and said:

"We have the greatest fighter in the world here tonight. He is going to show you what a boxer does to get in trim for a contest. Before he does, he will turn over $1,000 to anyone who can last through three rounds with him."

Kearns didn't think any person in the sellout gathering would actually fall for the offer, but he was sadly mistaken. One man, a six-foot shipyard worker, jumped to his feet and, in a gruff, loud voice, shouted to Kearns, "I'll take him on. I can lick yer champion."

Whereupon the din brought consternation to Kearns, who had to get out of the embarrassing situation. He hadn't figured on this. He stepped forth toward the challenger and said:

"Not tonight, my friend. Jack just finished a good, hearty meal. Come back tomorrow and Dempsey will be ready for you."

Hisses and boos greeted Kearns. The challenger wasn't permitting him to get away with it so easily. He started walking down the aisle with a chip on his shoulder. He insisted that Dempsey go through with the offer.

The huge gathering razzed Kearns until Dempsey appeared on the stage and started rope-skipping.

Dempsey finished that portion of his program and was about to start work on the big punching bag when the noisy gathering, with hand-clapping and stamping of feet, began yelling:

"Never mind that. We want the fight."

Kearns finally quieted the folks with the remark that Dempsey not only would face his tormentor the following night, but would knock his block off. Concluding, Kearns added:

"If you last three rounds, you'll not only get the $1,000, but I'll promise you an additional $5,000 and sign you to fight for me if you knock him down. I'll sign the contract right here so that all your friends can see it."

That brought cheers and sent the troublemaker back to his seat, though not entirely pacified.

The next night the challenger arrived with his boxing gloves and another shipyard worker, who was to act as his second.

The theater was packed. At 8:30, as previously arranged, the challenger came forward, wearing a sweater. He and his second were greeted by Kearns and Dempsey. Manassa Jack put his gloves on. Kearns supervised the show, making several announcements while the fighters were in their respective corners. Then Kearns introduced the shipbuilder and the champion.

Both received a hearty welcome, with that of the shipbuilder topping Jack's. The champion's tormentor stood in his corner, waving to friends and accepting the situation as one big jolly affair for him. As he came out of his corner to shake Dempsey's hand, he remarked:

"I'm gonna beat yer, champ."

Dempsey laughed. The bell clanged. Immediately Jack went into action. He rushed forth for a quick kill. His opponent had the same idea, but Jack was more accurate.

Manassa Jack sidestepped a left hook, then landed one on the jaw of the shipbuilder with such power it tossed him out of the ring into the orchestra pit, carrying with him several of the stakes to which the ropes of the makeshift ring were fastened. It was all over in a jiffy.

The people in the audience stood and cheered. This was the Dempsey they had heard so much about! They didn't get much action but they had seen what happens to those who crossed the champ's path.

The shipbuilder was quickly forgotten. But at least he could tell his friends that he had been in the same ring with Jack Dempsey.

13

DURING THE YEARS immediately following the victory over Willard, Dempsey says he was one of the most unpopular athletes in the country. People he never met displayed a dislike for him. He attributed it to the draft case, despite the fact that he was given a clean bill of health by his peers after a short trial in 1920. The situation affected Jack's popularity both in the movies and on the stage, and he felt it keenly. Yet the facts proved he deserved better treatment.

Dempsey was extremely conscious of the situation. He had achieved his goal of winning the world heavyweight crown. But he was still far from winning the confidence and goodwill of the public. And what Jack most cherished was public support for himself as the world heavyweight champion. This he was to gain, in part, with his triumph over the popular Frenchman, Georges Carpentier.

Let me review the cause of Dempsey's failure to gain public support for so long a period, a failure notwithstanding his station as the world's outstanding fighting man. Behind his unpopularity was the charge of slackerism during World War I. This charge irked him more than did his two defeats later at the hands of Gene Tunney, despite a quick jury verdict in his favor.

I was close to Jack from the start of his Eastern invasion in 1916 and have always insisted that he was caused to suffer unjustly. He was steered from entering the armed forces through bad advice. He was eager to join the army; twice he tried to enlist, but was turned down.

The draft charge was a messy affair for which I blame jealousy. I followed the case closely. I was a Dempsey confidant and never did believe he was guilty of evading an issue so vital to all of us during the hectic war period. His greatest blunder was permitting himself to be photographed in the Philadelphia shipyards in 1918 in his best clothes, wearing patent-leather shoes and spats with a pair of shiny overalls covering well-pressed trousers.

For that blunder he blamed Kearns and the overenthusiastic photographer, who was so eager to obtain the picture. The photo was responsible for considerable harm. It brought ridicule, abuse, and hatred that lasted for several years, despite Dempsey's speedy acquittal. The affair was undignified and a terrible error for which Kearns, not Dempsey, was to blame.

At the trial, the naval officer in charge of the Great Lakes Station testified he had informed Dempsey that his services were far more beneficial in the recruiting field and in the selling of Liberty Bonds, and that it would be a gross error for Jack to enter the armed forces. That testimony weighed heavily in the quick verdict delivered in Jack's favor.

The officer declared that faulty advice, not a desire to shirk his duty, was responsible for Jack's plight. That was evident when in World War II, despite a turndown by several branches of the armed forces, Manassa Jack joined the Coast Guard, where his services gained several thousand recruits for his outfit. He was accorded special recognition for his efforts from his superiors.

It was on June 7, 1920, that Dempsey went on trial in the U.S. District Court in San Francisco on the draft-evasion charge. He was accused of swearing falsely that his parents, wife, and brothers were dependent on his support, as a result of which he received a deferred classification. The indictment against Jack was strange, considering that two brothers, Joseph and Johnny —the latter, the younger, had undergone three operations— were in poor health and each was given limited service by the draft board.

At the trial, Rudolph Goodman, a Chicago notary who had witnessed Jack's signature to a questionnaire, testified that Kearns answered all the questions and Dempsey approved the answers. In his declaration, Dempsey said that his ex-wife, Maxine Cates, was unable to work and depended on him, and that he contributed toward the support of his parents and his widowed sister and her children.

After the government's case was closed, Maxine testified against her former husband. But the testimony of Jack's mother was far different. She told how her son, since he was 14 years old, helped sustain the family. In 1917 and 1918, he sent money to her regularly, she told the court. She said that for many years her husband had been crippled with rheumatism and that she was ill for many months. It was stated in the testimony that Jack's sister, Mrs. Effie Clarkson, had undergone several operations and that brother Bruce, when 16 years old, was stabbed to death in 1917. Bruce was the baby of the family.

Jack was the family's principal support, said his mother. His brothers had married and had families of their own. She told of sums Jack had sent home regularly and that, after the fight with Willard, Jack bought a $20,000 home for the family.

After Mama Dempsey had completed her testimony, Jack took the stand. He told how he was his family's chief support from the time he was 14. He detailed his farm work, then told of his mining experiences, his work as a carpenter, and, finally, his work as a fighter. Jack declared he had earned about $4,000 in 1917, most of which he contributed to his family. He declared that he spent the following year in patriotic benefits for which he received no pay but for which he was given a gold pencil and a watch. Asked whether his opponents were paid, Jack answered in the negative; he did state, however, that Willard had received $30,000 for an appearance in Chicago.

Dempsey said he supported his ex-wife, despite her previous testimony to the contrary. He declared this had continued until she deserted him. He denied breaking her jaw, as she had testified. He said the fracture was caused by a fall.

Jack said that he left his wife in San Francisco in 1917, went to Salt Lake City to box, then returned two days later to find his wife gone. He said she went to live with her brother. Dempsey then told of his wife's travels to Yakima, Washington, to see her mother. His wife, he said, failed to return to him. Cross-examination failed to shake him.

Jack told the court that he and Kearns had signed draft papers in Larry Lichtenstein's room in Chicago. The last named was a manager and a promoter.

Dempsey declared that twice he tried to enlist, but Lieutenant Kennard of the battleship *Mississippi* had waited too long to sign the necessary documents. The enlistment was halted by order of the Secretary of the Navy while Jack was on his way to Philadelphia.

After being quickly cleared, Jack remarked, "I'm glad it's over. The trial has given me an absolutely clean bill. I was not a slacker. I tried to enlist but it was blocked. I was deferred due to my having to support my family. That's why I engaged in about 40 boxing bouts in various parts of the country raising funds for the Red Cross. I netted upwards of $200,000. Barring the doughboys, I don't see anyone in my circumstances who gave more freely of personal services. I was called a slacker. I never was. I knew I'd be acquitted."

The fact that Dempsey was able to live down the slacker charge has been one of his greatest achievements.

14

HAVING REACHED THE TOP of the ladder, but with little money to show for Dempsey's efforts, Kearns decided to take the champion to California in 1920. Both he and Dempsey had been very active for a long time and the manager figured a rest period would do each a lot of good.

As arrangements for the trip were being made, Kearns received word from Tex Rickard that negotiations for a fight between Manassa Jack and Georges Carpentier had been started. Tex told Kearns that he had been in communication with Francois Deschamps, the Frenchman's manager, and that he was bringing him and Carpentier to New York to discuss a title bout with Dempsey.

"I need your help," said Rickard.

Rickard told Kearns to keep Dempsey ready. Kearns was elated. He told Rickard that a fight with Carpentier was what both he and Dempsey wanted most.

"I'll call Jack and tell him what you're doing. I'll try to keep him busy until we know definitely whether the Frenchman is willing to go along with us."

"That's not necessary," Tex replied. "Deschamps is just as eager for the fight as we are, but he has a number of people in England with whom he must discuss the plans before anything can be arranged."

With that information, Kearns was now satisfied that a bout with Carpentier could be clinched and he headed for California to discuss these matters with Dempsey, who had gone on ahead of him.

In discussing the preliminary meeting with me, Kearns said that he was elated. It was what both he and Dempsey most desired—a fight for the heavyweight crown with Carpentier as the challenger. His greatest fear, however, was that Dempsey might go stale.

"I went to California," said Kearns, "to make certain that would not happen. My champ was a restless fellow and needed some work to keep up his spirits. So I took him to Los Angeles for a three-round exhibition with Terry Keller, whom Jack had stopped in 1918. That exhibition proved to me that Jack was in good condition and stopped me from worrying."

Kearns went all out in quest of the fortune he had promised Dempsey if he was successful in winning the Willard bout. No time was wasted. Kearns kept close to Rickard. The negotiations for the Carpentier were progressing.

While waiting for Carpentier's mentor to make a decision, Kearns decided on a few more tune-ups for the Manassa Mauler to keep him in top shape. Kearns arranged to pit Dempsey against Billy Miske. Billy had fought Dempsey twice, one a ten-round no-decision affair that went the limit, in St. Paul, Minnesota, on May 3, 1918; the other, a no-decision bout of six rounds in Philadelphia on November 28, 1918.

Now Miske was ill. He was suffering from Bright's disease but kept his ailment a secret while attempting to obtain funds for his family. He had been warned by his physician to give up boxing, but Billy ignored the warning and continued fighting.

Dempsey knew that Billy had been ill, but was unaware of the nature of the disease from which he was suffering. After considerable pleas, Kearns agreed to a third bout, following a special meeting with his friend, Floyd Fitzsimmons, a promoter who had secretly informed Dempsey's manager of Miske's plight.

"He needs our help badly," pleaded Floyd. "Let's give him a helping hand. He's poor both financially and in health. Let's help."

Kearns agreed. Both he and Dempsey were eager to give their friend the aid he sought. The bout was arranged. It was set for September 6, 1920, Labor Day, at Benton Harbor, Michigan, a contest in which Manassa Jack scored a knockout in the third round.

Their initial contest, in St. Paul, was at a time when Miske was at his best. He was a good, thrill-providing fighter and the affair was well received. In the third round, Miske aroused his followers to wild enthusiasm with a left to the stomach that had Dempsey in distress. The bell brought sweet music to Jack's ear.

In the seventh round, Dempsey clouted Billy with a left to the stomach that caused Billy to wince. He saved himself by clinching.

Jack struck Miske a low blow twice in the fourth round, but Billy made no complaint, although Dempsey did complain when Billy hit below the belt in the second round.

In their second encounter, Miske was outclassed. When the final gong sounded, Billy was a thoroughly beaten man. He had been doubled up several times by vicious body punishment but Billy saved himself by clinching. At times he held on with what appeared to be the tenacity of a shipwrecked sailor.

Referee Lou Grimson became exhausted tearing Billy away during the clinches. He was unaware that Billy was then suffering from an incurable disease.

Almost two years after that bout, Manassa Jack and Miske engaged in their third match. This time Dempsey was the heavyweight king and his opponent—though Jack's title was at stake—was facing the Manassa Mauler for the sole purpose of obtaining sufficient aid for his family, knowing his chances to win the world crown were virtually nil.

Kearns and Floyd Fitzsimmons had agreed that Jim Dougherty would referee, but at ring time, the boxing commission objected to the choice. Chairman Bigger was determined that a local referee would handle the fight, but after considerable discussion, Dougherty was given the assignment.

Benton Harbor was in an uproar during the delay in naming the third man in the ring. The fans were put at ease with the naming of Dougherty.

The fight was one of the easiest Manassa Jack had ever engaged in. Miske, at this stage of his career, was no longer capable of giving a good account of himself.

A right to the jaw brought Miske down for a nine-count in the third round. He was in distress throughout that frame. He had been badly hurt by body punches in the opening round and was suffering severe pain.

The punch that started him on the road to a knockout was a vicious right to the body in the final canto. It caused Billy to grunt. He winced in pain. He was badly hurt. The blow robbed Billy of everything but his gameness.

Miske was first knocked down in the opening round when Dempsey sank a deep right under Billy's heart. Miske dropped like a log.

He was sprawled on the canvas and in distress. His face was distorted as he started to get up. He was aided somewhat by the referee who thought Billy wanted to quit.

The bell came to Miske's rescue. He shuffled to his corner where his seconds worked feverishly over him. When the bell clanged, Miske came out of his corner to face his tormentor again.

As Dempsey came forward, Miske let go a perfect right and it landed with force on Dempsey's jaw. It was the best punch Jack's opponent had tossed during the fight.

The blow caused Dempsey's knees to buckle but he quickly recovered his equilibrium, backed away, then tore in after his prey. It was Miske's last stand. From that point on the challenger was at Dempsey's mercy.

In the final frame, Dempsey stood calmly in his corner while Referee Dougherty, following a conference with Miske, decided to permit the affair to continue.

At the resumption of activities, Dempsey, surly-looking as always when he faced an opponent, advanced toward Billy and let go a right. It missed, going over Billy's head. Then followed another right, which crashed with power against Billy's jaw.

Miske dropped, with his right arm curled under his head. He was badly hurt. He lay on the canvas helpless while the referee counted him out. Several of his ribs were badly bruised, as was his jaw.

Dempsey, with the aid of Dougherty and one of Miske's handlers, raised Billy and helped him to his chair where he remained for a time before leaving for his dressing room.

The fight was an amazing one considering the poor condition of the challenger. But most important, Billy had accomplished what he had set out to do—bring aid to his family. He received as his share of the receipts a check for $25,000 from a gate of $134,904, which state and federal taxes had reduced to $109,476. Dempsey received $55,000. For this fight Manassa Jack weighed 188; Miske tilted the scales at 175½.

After the knockout, Kearns and Dempsey made an invasion of the East. Kearns was riled at the failure to bring into his partnership with Dempsey the money he figured on obtaining in his new role as manager of a great fighter. He needed another *big* fight—and soon.

15

NOW, MORE THAN EVER, Kearns, with a title as the bartering basis, was out to get the popular Carpentier to the United States to do battle with Dempsey. Rickard likewise was on the trail of the Frenchman. Both Tex and Kearns realized the value of a bout between Manassa Jack and handsome Georges. It would furnish the outstanding sports event of the decade. Plans, already in motion, were speeded up to clinch this match for the United States.

However, things were not working too smoothly for Kearns. He found Rickard as shrewd as ever. While Kearns realized he had a firm grip on the best drawing card in pugilism, he also was aware that Rickard's skill as a promoter and his friendship with the money men of Wall Street were not to be ignored.

Now, with the Carpentier match looming, Kearns decided to follow Rickard's admonition to stick to the management of the champion and let Tex tend to the promoting. Three months after the knockout of Miske in Benton Harbor, Dempsey appeared in the old Madison Square Garden in a bout with Bill Brennan.

Their first engagement had taken place in Milwaukee, February 25, 1918, with Jack putting his opponent away in the sixth round. By now, Brennan had gained considerable experience, having engaged in many tough battles. His manager, Leo P. Flynn, was confident that Bill, one of the many heavyweights seeking a shot at the title, had an excellent chance of whipping the Manassa Mauler. But it didn't turn out that way. Dempsey's power punches proved too much to overcome.

On December 14, 1920, the return contest between Brennan and Dempsey took place for the world heavyweight title. On this occasion, unlike their first encounter, the end of the battle came six rounds later, in the 12th, with Manassa Jack again the victor by a knockout. The termination of this contest was welcomed by each. It came at 1:57 of the 12th round, with Brennan lying in agony on the canvas, the victim of three explosive punches.

It was a left hook to Bill's stomach that started him on the road to defeat. Brennan doubled up in pain and Dempsey quickly followed with a well-directed right, delivered with all the power he could summon. The punch struck the side of Bill's head. As the challenger was going down, Dempsey landed another right, this time to the victim's unguarded left side. Then Brennan dropped on hands and knees and Referee Billy Haukop began the toll.

At the count of seven, Bill was part way up. Then he suddenly fell flat and was counted out. He got to his feet just after Haukop completed the count.

Dempsey didn't realize that he had knocked out his opponent. There were many in the vast Garden throng who were of the opinion that the referee had halted the bout because of Brennan's condition, but Haukop officially announced that Bill had been knocked out.

The affair was replete with sensational events. More than once it appeared that Brennan would bring home the bacon. Although Bill had been floored in both the first round and the second, several times in the first ten rounds it appeared that he might succeed in driving home the winning punch. It was not until the sixth that Manassa Jack became effective. It was an uphill battle for Dempsey.

In the second, Bill shot a power blow to Dempsey's chin and followed with a powerful uppercut that jarred the champ. Jack was groggy. His legs were wobbly. Brennan was as surprised as his opponent. Bill stepped back and foolishly looked at Dempsey. That hesitation enabled the champion to regain his senses and proved costly to Brennan. Dempsey quickly stepped into a clinch to recover.

For the remainder of the round he and his opponent exchanged blows. From that round through the fifth, Dempsey's usual tearing-in tactics and rushes were missing. He blamed it on the power sock to the jaw he had received in the second round.

Dempsey's judgment of distance that night was poor. He often missed. In comparison, Brennan was at his best. He realized he couldn't play with his opponent. Hence at times when he had Dempsey cornered, he cut loose and forced Jack to clinch.

In the sixth the champ went after his prey. Fighting in his usual crouching style, Dempsey struck often and with punishing power.

Throughout most of the battle, the challenger was content to wait for openings through which he often crashed his right cross and uppercut. The fans cheered as Dempsey was clouted. The majority of the spectators apparently were Brennan rooters.

Brennan's defense was good. He kept his jaw well guarded and body out of reach during most of the first half of the battle.

In the eighth, Dempsey came forth with a rush. He knew he was behind and decided to make up lost ground. Kearns was urging him on. A right to Brennan's jaw rocked the challenger. It appeared he might go down, but kept erect by clinching. That punch was a power clout that proved to Dempsey the challenger was still in possession of his faculties. It put Jack on guard.

Following a brief spell of infighting, Dempsey cut loose. He crashed a blow to the side of Brennan's face. Had it landed flush, it probably would have downed the challenger. As it was, Brennan was stunned by the punch.

Dempsey was now out for the kill. He knew that unless he stopped Brennan, the decision might go against him.

In the 12th, Brennan rocked Jack with several well-aimed shots. The champ was bleeding. But suddenly he came alive and went all out to put his game, determined opponent away before another round got under way.

As they came out of a clinch, Dempsey sank a beauty of a left hook into Brennan's breadbasket, doubling up the challenger. A right to the head immediately followed. Bill was stunned. His legs sagged and his body was bent over. One more right, to the ribs, and the fight was history.

Dempsey weighed in at 187½; Brennan tipped the scales at 197.

The contest was one of the top bouts seen in the heavyweight division in the old Garden's final years. Joe Humphreys, clarion-voiced announcer, stepped into the ring at the end of the bout and, with Rickard at his side, presented to Dempsey a diamond-studded belt, emblematic of the world heavyweight championship.

16

FUNDS WERE GETTING LOW. Kearns and his fighter were big spenders. And to add to their problems, they were being harassed in many cities by veterans associations whose members continued to harp on the draft-evasion charges, of which Dempsey had been cleared.

Kearns and Dempsey were increasingly certain that a fight with Carpentier would check the harassment, as well as add substantially to their coffers. But they were becoming impatient with the delays in commencing serious negotiations for a Carpentier match.

At last, Carpentier and his manager, Francois Deschamps, arrived in New York, coming at the invitation of Rickard. Georges had served in World War I and was very popular. Both Rickard and Kearns realized that Deschamps must be convinced that a Dempsey-Carpentier bout would be the biggest sports event of the year.

Negotiations, serious ones, quickly got under way. Tex and Kearns knew their task was not an easy one. There were other international figures with whom the promoter would have to do business besides the wily Deschamps, one of the shrewdest fight managers of the era.

Francois was fully aware of the deep interest in a Dempsey-Carpentier match. He knew also of Rickard's anxiety to sign the match. Accordingly, Deschamps decided to play his hand to the limit. The "French Fox" believed he could obtain the guarantee he figured Carpentier was worth.

Rickard was a man of action, skilled in the fight game, and fully acquainted with its intricacies. Tex was doubtless as shrewd a promoter as ever had come to the front. For some time he had combed the field in search of an opponent to oppose Dempsey in a title fight, an opponent who he figured could obtain the wholehearted support of the public.

Rickard envisioned a great international match. He saw the ideal challenger as a top popular boxer from abroad, one who, as it were, would storm the States in quest of the heavyweight crown. The man he had long had in mind was Carpentier.

Secretly Tex had made a trip abroad. He had his contacts in England. Through them he hoped to sign the Frenchman as Dempsey's next opponent. It was to be an arduous task. But what Rickard went after, he usually landed.

It was in the latter part of September 1920 that the American public first became aware of Rickard's intentions. It was learned that for some months Tex had been busy planning a world title contest between Carpentier and Manassa Jack. Negotiations that had been carried on secretly were now on the verge of completion. Dempsey's triumph over Miske and the expected one over Brennan had paved the way for Rickard's latest move. Now Tex would spare no effort in bringing those secret negotiations to successful completion. He was certain he had the principals to bring off the first million-dollar gate in boxing history. He was not about to let them slip away.

Carpentier, the French idol, was the glamour boy of pugilism. Managed by Francois Deschamps, Georges had come up through the ranks from the lowest level. He was good-looking and very astute.

The shrewd Deschamps knew the ropes and played his cards well during negotiations for the fight. Rickard's enterprise at Toledo was a piker's job compared with what he now faced in making the Dempsey-Carpentier match. The undertaking had no parallel in ring history.

Preliminary details were settled to the satisfaction of Deschamps, after which Rickard named two others who would act with him in the promotion. They were William A. Brady, a New York theatrical impresario who in years past had managed both James J. Jeffries and James J. Corbett, and Charles B. Cochran, a British theatrical producer and sports promoter.

On November 5, 1920, they met in the Claridge Hotel, a sports rendezvous in Times Square. At a special session with reporters, Rickard announced that an agreement had been reached and that articles would soon be signed by Deschamps and Kearns on behalf of their fighters.

Since that could not be done in New York, where the law prohibited it, Rickard declared that it would be accomplished in New Jersey. Accordingly, the promoter, accompanied by Ike Dorgan (press representative), Kearns, Deschamps, and the lawyers, took a ferry ride across the Hudson River to Weehawken, New Jersey, where signatures were affixed to the contracts.

Among those who witnessed the signing was Bob Edgren, the stakeholder. The document carried no locality where the bout must be staged, but an approximate date was set—between May 29 and July 4, 1921. The number of rounds was to be between 10 and 15, based on the location.

It was stipulated that Dempsey was to receive $300,000 and Carpentier, $200,000. In addition, each was to receive a 25 percent interest in the picture rights, with the remaining 50 percent held by the promoters. It was also stipulated that the fighters would have the privilege of a percentage: 36 percent for Dempsey and 24 for Carpentier.

The contract also provided that each of the contestants must deposit $50,000 by November 20 as forfeit money.

Other clauses to protect the fighters were to be incorporated at a later time. Regardless of what might happen, if the terms of the agreement were not met, the fighters were to receive their purses, paid in full.

As a result of the insertion of the clause pertaining to the forfeit money, Cochran threatened to quit. He was opposed to the plan.

The names of Otto Floto, James J. Corbett, James J. Jeffries, Bob Edgren, James Dougherty, and Bill Brown, famous New York referee and physical-culture instructor, were listed in the agreement as possible officials. All were acceptable.

Now came the big headache for Rickard. A vicious attack was launched against him and the proposed fight by the American Legion, and by members of the House of Representatives and the United States Senate. Patriotic organizations from many parts of the country also objected. The American Legion denounced the spending of so much money on a prizefight while thousands of wounded servicemen were unable to obtain the aid they required. They attacked Dempsey's draft role, and called the entire affair most unpatriotic.

Rickard ignored the uproar. He was urged by Cochran to take the fight to London, but Tex replied that it would not be taken outside the United States. Whereupon Cochran quit the combine.

The forfeit money, which Kearns and Deschamps were to deposit in a United States bank under the agreement with Rickard, next came up for discussion. Deschamps had placed his forfeit money in a French bank, but Kearns was holding out. Cochran's share had been placed in the Union Trust Company of New York, but was withdrawn when he quit the combine.

Cochran then declared he would take the fight to London.

Brady, angered by the entire procedure, withdrew his support, thus leaving the entire responsibility in Rickard's hands.

Tex requested Kearns to change his financial demands, but the latter refused. It was then that Rickard took in as a silent partner his friend John Ringling, who later joined Tex in building the new Madison Square Garden. Rickard sent a message to Deschamps, now in France, telling him of the proceedings, and received his okay. The fight was now definitely arranged.

Rickard built a huge wooden arena in Jersey City that was named Boyle's Thirty Acres. The arena's seating capacity was 91,613. The ultimate success of the venture proved that Rickard was a genius, as 80,183 paid their way in for a total gross of $1,789,238.

In order to obtain public support for this gigantic undertaking, Rickard had no objection to Kearns' request for funds to go all out in obtaining support for so huge a venture. Tex himself tossed a number of parties for reporters to start the buildup. He held frequent news conferences. I was one of his confidants at the time and did considerable advance word with Ike Dorgan, his press representative, in the initial buildup. Ike later became my partner in the ownership of *The Ring.*

When Carpentier and his entourage took up residence in training quarters at Manhasset, Long Island, a number of reporters decided to call on Georges for his first interview. When they got to his quarters, they found a cordon of special police on guard. They informed the newsmen that they had been given instructions not to permit any reporters to enter the camp.

The writers protested vigorously but to no avail. The purpose seemed obvious. The camp was to be kept free of reporters because Deschamps and his aide, Jack Curley, were fully aware that the Frenchman's appearance before the inquiring eyes of the press would not meet with approval.

The act created quite a commotion. The reporters cussed, fumed, threatened—but they couldn't gain admittance. They appealed to Rickard, explaining that they had a job to perform. Bill McBeth of the *New York Herald* led the brigade.

To help out the newsmen, Jack Curley said he would get the answers to all questions placed in writing for them, but this did not meet with approval.

"When can we see him and discuss his plans?" asked Frank Graham of the *Sun.*

"I have no idea," replied Curley. "I'm following my instructions."

The newsmen, including my boxing expert, George B. Underwood of the *New York Press,* Graham, McBeth, and a dozen others, were flabbergasted at the treatment. Chagrined, the reporters left the camp vowing to even the score.

The sports pages the following day lambasted the French group. Rickard, sensing trouble, called a news session at which he promised he would have matters changed for the press. The following day all were made welcome.

In the *New York Press,* of which I was sports editor, I placed the following head over Underwood's story:

Throughout the training period, the Frenchman trotted out for a public inspection only a few times. His true fighting form was hidden from both the press and the public. That unfavorable reports in the press were warranted became obvious on the day of the fight, when Georges met his master.

Two weeks before the contest, the time, according to the contracts, to select a referee, Kearns informed the boxing commission that one of the six originally named must be the choice.

"Not so," was the terse reply of Commissioner Charles Lyons, head of the New Jersey Boxing Commission. "We are in charge here and we will choose the official without your help," he informed Kearns.

That started a new rumpus. Rickard and Kearns, angered at the turn of affairs, declared that the third man in the ring must be one of the six chosen and agreed upon when the contracts were signed.

"This is our territory," answered Lyons. "We run the show. The referee will be chosen by my commission without outside help."

That's how it finally was decided. There was too much at stake to carry out any threats. Commissioner Lyons knew that Kearns and Rickard would not jeopardize their huge financial interests by acting against the commission's decision.

After a short hassle, Lyons announced he had decided on having New Jersey's top official, Harry Ertle, supervise the fight. He was a competent official and no further objection was raised.

The stage was finally cleared for the international contest.

That is, it was nearly cleared. It was on June 29 that Rickard, after a conference with Deschamps and Kearns, broke the news that he had set aside $500,000 for the payment of the fighters in lieu of the 36 percent to Dempsey and the 24 percent to Carpentier, as was originally decided. It would be a straight payment with no percentage.

At first there were considerable objections by both managers, but they finally acquiesced. Kearns never forgave Rickard for what he termed trickery. It proved to be a costly blunder by the managers and a plum for Rickard.

At the time Tex pulled off the deal, neither Kearns nor Deschamps was aware of the huge advance sale and that the bout would eventually wind up with a million-dollar gate. For this fight, Rickard had plans never before dreamed of by any promoter. He proved in this contest, more so than in any other he staged, that he was a man of vision.

The *New York Times* had hired Irvin S. Cobb, famous author, to cover the bout. In his first article he wrote:

"The arts, sciences, drama, politics, commerce, and the new bootlegging industry all have sent their pink, their pick, and their perfection to grace the great occasion. The names of the occupants of ringside seats would sound like the reading of the first hundred pages of 'Who's Ballyhoo in America.' "

Through a hundred entrances the multitude steadily and smoothly flowed to their seats. "If it takes all sorts to make up the world, the world must be here already," opined Rickard, grinning broadly.

It was a day crammed with thrills for Rickard.

"I never *seed* anything like it," he kept repeating as he greeted reporters.

They were standing at the threshold of a boxing first—the million-dollar gate. More would follow.

Incidentally, the man who fought Dempsey in two such extravaganzas, Gene Tunney, appeared on the undercard. He faced Soldier Jones in the semifinal and knocked him out in the seventh round. It was in the Carpentier fight, according to Gene, that he saw the faults in Dempsey's fighting style which enabled him to defeat Jack in their two engagements.

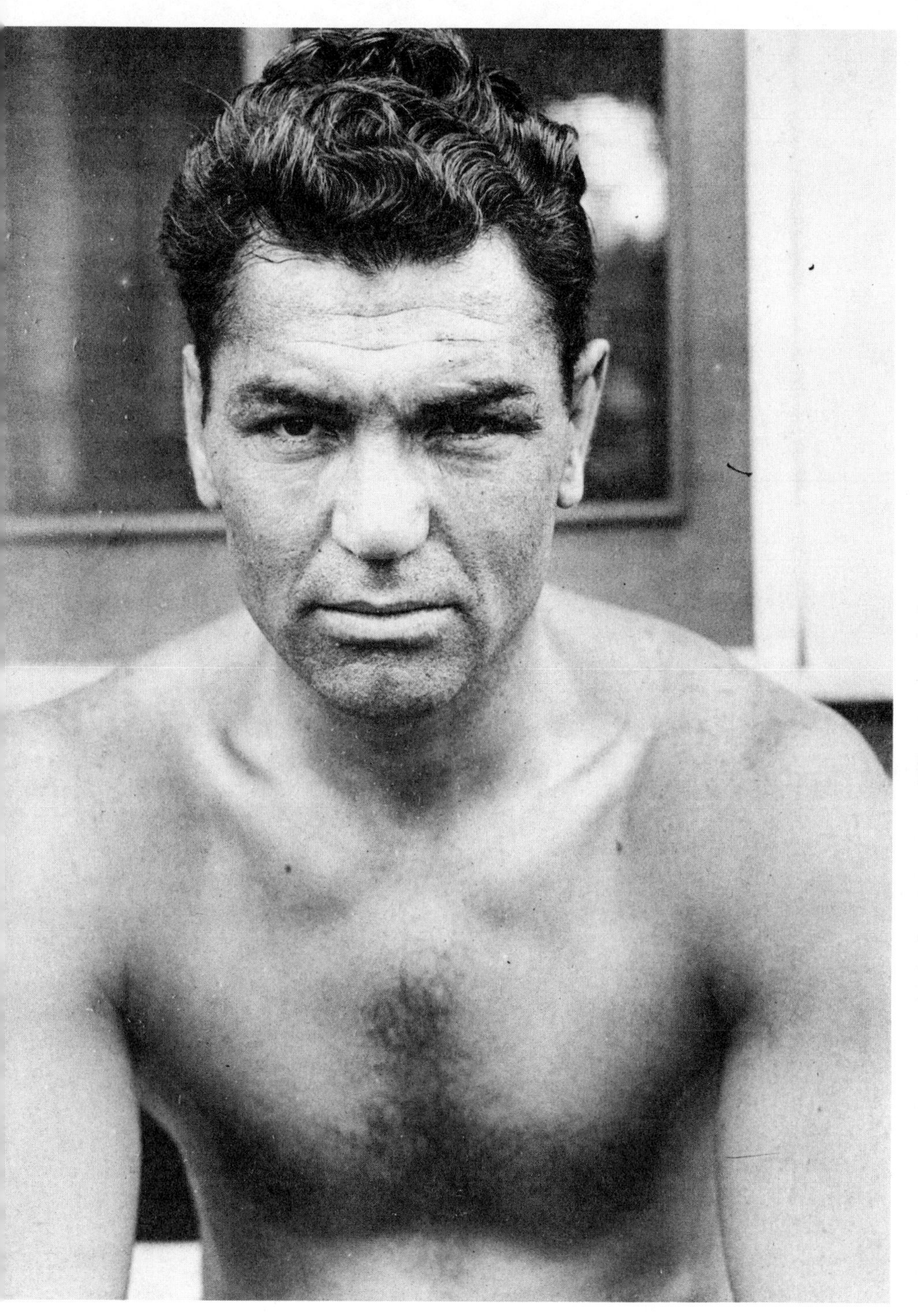

Close-up of Manassa Jack in his heyday.

Jack tickles the ivories to entertain his entourage and to break up the training camp grind.

Contracts are about to be signed for the Dempsey-Carpentier fight, boxing's first million-dollar gate. Left to right, *seated:* Dempsey, William A. Brady, Charles Cochran, Tex Rickard, Georges Carpentier, Francois Deschamps; *standing:* Jack Kearns, Charles Lyons, Bob Edgren, Harry Hechheimer, Captain Mallet, Nathan Vidane.

Carpentier (left) and his manager, Francois Deschamps, taking a breather at their Manhasset, Long Island, training camp in 1921, shortly before the bout with Dempsey.

About to sail for Europe, Jack gets a goodbye kiss from noted dancer Florence Walton.

Dempsey puts finishing touches on makeup for the silent film *Daredevil Jack,* in which he starred in Hollywood.

A shot of what little action occurred during Dempsey's 15-round title defense against Tom Gibbons (dark trunks) at Shelby, Montana, July 4, 1923.

Dempsey stares at camera as New York State Athletic Commissioner William Muldoon adjusts scales at weigh-in for Firpo bout. Nat Fleischer is at left in light topcoat. Two others not identified.

17

FOR SOME, the great moment that afternoon of July 2, 1921, came in round four, when Carpentier, battered, fell like a broken lily to the gleaming white canvas. For others, those who saw the drama of life in the bloody but unbowed head of the loser, the second round was the thrill-provider.

In the opening round, Dempsey had worked his punishing body blows to perfection in the clinches. He whipped in short, snappy destructive wallops until the challenger's midsection showed pink under the beating.

Realizing he was facing a tiger man, Carpentier went forth in the second session to cut loose with all the fury he possessed in an all-out attempt at a quick victory. He leaped from his chair at the sound of the gong and went after the Manassa Mauler with all the vim his 175 pounds could muster. He was brilliant.

The 80,000-plus were astir. Was the Frenchman with a fighting heart about to dethrone the American champ? The atmosphere was charged with expectancy. To no avail. Georges couldn't nail the champ. He made a game effort, but it was his last.

In the third, Dempsey stopped the Orchid Man's advances by means of close-range battling. The way was now being paved for the climax by means of a series of well-directed attacks on the body. They sapped the vitality and stamina of the Frenchman until it no longer was possible for the tricolor war hero to withstand the punishment.

His seconds advised him to make a running fight of it, but it was too late. The damage had been done. Jack had whipped Georges' body badly in that frame.

Then came the fatal fourth. It took only a little time for Dempsey to corner his foe. He backed him against the ropes and feinted for an opening.

In a moment when the French idol's jaw was unguarded, the champion's deadly right found its mark and the foe slipped limply to the canvas. Georges was hurt.

The great roar that had accompanied the assault suddenly receded. Stillness swept over the arena. The throng leaned forward, watching the intense drama.

In the silence, Referee Ertle, dressed in white, kept raising his arm, tolling off the seconds. Opposite him was another occupant of the ring. Fists cocked, body tense, arms shaking, rarin' to be let loose, Dempsey stood awaiting the "kill."

At the count of nine, Carpentier, with a heroic effort, got to his feet. The sinewy figure of Dempsey leaped forward with the speed of a hungry mountain lion. A vicious left uppercut struck Georges with force. Then a right above the heart. The Frenchman staggered, in pain. His knees bent forward, his arms fell slowly to his sides, his body sagged.

Dempsey, taut, stood looking at his foe. Then he swished a terrific right through the air that sent his opponent hurtling to the floor.

Ten seconds later, America still was the possessor of the world heavyweight crown.

This fight, an international contest, was a milestone, the most important fight up to that time. The $1,789,238 in gate receipts made boxing a big business—and enabled Rickard to convince Wall Street that a new Madison Square Garden would be a paying venture. When in 1925 the new Garden was opened to the public, many looked back four years to the bout in Boyle's Thirty Acres, where Dempsey and the Frenchman had drawn the first million-dollar gate in any sport, anywhere! And with the million-dollar gate came the "nice people," as Rickard was wont to call his patrons.

Also marking this as a red-letter day were the two firsts chalked up by the radio industry: the first fight to be broadcast in the United States—a preliminary on the Dempsey-Carpentier card; and the first broadcast of a world championship. Major Andrew White was at the controls and I was his assistant.

Kearns' part in bringing the million-dollar gate to pugilism cannot be overlooked. Master publicist, king of the ballyhoo artists, Kearns was as much responsible for the emergence of the fistic extravaganza as was Rickard.

The contestants who drew boxing's first million-dollar gate have remained close friends over the decades. Each has visited the other. Shortly after the liberation of France in World War II, Dempsey entered Paris as a commander in the United States Coast Guard. On seeing Manassa Jack, Carpentier wept, then kissed and embraced his old adversary.

July 2, 1921. A great day. A gallant fight.

"I never *seed* anything like it."

18

As a result of the Carpentier contest, Dempsey found his popularity on the rise. What with his previous problems, this was a new experience for him, one which he enjoyed immensely. To capitalize on this situation, both Dempsey and Kearns decided to tour the country and make public appearances. For nearly two years they roamed from city to city, appearing in theaters and engaging in an occasional exhibition to keep the champ fresh. Those who found the champ's fistic skills in good working order were Elziar Rioux (an expectant Montreal crowd watched Rioux go down for the count in the first), Jack Renault, Andre Anderson, and Jack Thompson.

During the tour Kearns' old desire to do his own promoting was awakened in him. He talked it over with Dempsey. Kearns, as usual, was all for action. The time was ripe, so he reasoned. The Fates now took a hand in the proceedings.

The place was Shelby, Montana, on a cold January night in 1923. A group of prospectors were whooping it up in one of the saloons, despite Congressman Volstead and his prohibition law.

Several natives had assembled around a few bottles of Scotch. Heads together, they were working out a scheme to let the world know what a great place Shelby was and what a fine future lay ahead for it.

Shelby had struck oil in 1921. At the time, it was a little cowtown in north central Montana with a population of about 500. Prior to the discovery of oil, Shelby was listed as one of the poorest towns in the Midwest. A few sheepherders, cowboys, and dirt farmers, all striving for an existence, made up the population. It was a town on the Montana desert where the Far West begins, and where the natives had little money.

The plan that was hatched called for a heavyweight title bout for July 4, 1923, to lure more prospectors. Each subscriber was to receive a ringside seat. Those who concocted the scheme kept it a secret until they were satisfied it could be successfully carried out. But it was a dream that was to turn into a nightmare.

Sam Sampson was chosen to manage the venture. He sent wires to Kearns and Dempsey, but received no response. In desperation he called for help. He sent for Mike Collins, nationally known promoter, sportswriter, and publisher of a boxing magazine.

Collins arrived in Shelby on March 15, 1923, at which time he was met by interested parties. He found that Shelby consisted of a few houses, a garage, the Silver Grill Cafe, a couple of small hotels, some saloons, three rooming houses, the Great Northern depot, a mountain on one side, an oil field on another, and the Great Northern Railroad running east and west.

Collins was flabbergasted! He asked, after surveying his surroundings, "What's up?"

"Why?" asked Sampson.

"Well," replied Collins, "the idea alone would make you all the laughingstock of the country. A little cowtown with a population of about 500 trying to outbid cities of several million for the big attraction you say you want."

"We can do it," was the crisp answer he received.

The following morning there was a meeting of the citizens who were going to raise the money to stage the proposed title bout. Mose Zimmerman of St. Paul, Minnesota, who at the time owned most of the new Shelby townside and was reselling it at a huge profit, was slated to furnish $300,000 to stage the show.

But when the time arrived for the ten o'clock meeting, Mose did not appear. When located, he inquired:

"Are you men crazy? What are you trying to do?"

Collins left the meeting in disgust and decided to go home. He wondered how the people of so small a town could become involved in so huge a financial venture.

But Collins couldn't get away. He was requested to join John Dwyer and Carl Schwartz, prominent merchants, at a meeting in the Town Hall. When they arrived they found the place jammed. A cheer rent the air when Collins reached the platform to discuss the affair with inhabitants and visitors.

The spokesman for the town fathers insisted that the fathers wanted a Dempsey–Tommy Gibbons match to be staged in Shelby on Independence Day and Collins was requested to handle it. In reviewing this phase of the proceedings, Collins recalled, "I advised those behind the project that we needed $100,000 within two days to start the ball rolling and another $100,000 ten days later.

" 'Get the money up to show good faith,' I told them, 'and I'll work with you.'

"In the next 20 minutes, $20,000 was raised. Vouchers were given for the amount and all the money was on the table before the meeting was over. The folks asked me to wire Kearns and Eddie Kane, manager of Gibbons. This I did. Eight days later, I had the balance, and now had assurance that the fight would go on as proposed."

Loy B. Molumby, state commander of the American Legion, and Collins visited most of the state by airplane and auto. They gave more than three dozen talks before Rotary clubs, civic and commerce associations, and Kiwanis organizations. They obtained $110,000 for the Shelby venture. That was before any of the principals had signed for the fight. Ringside seats were promised to each subscriber.

Collins then went to Chicago where he met the two managers, Kearns and Kane. On May 5, articles were signed. The fight was now assured.

But there was no arena. Nor was there money for the construction of one. Every citizen of Shelby had plenty of empty lots and they were offered for the promotion. After four days of wrangling, Jim Johnson, mayor of Shelby, was elected treasurer. An arena to seat 40,000 was started on credit. The concessions were sold for $200,000.

Several days before the fight, the owners of the lumber being used for the arena threatened to seize the site and stop the show unless paid. However, when Major Lane, the man who furnished the lumber, was chosen president of the fight group, he calmed down. All was well again.

The ballyhoo, once under way, brought many visitors to Shelby, among them a small flock of fly-by-night promoters, plus scores of opportunists interested in exploiting the oil strike. Shelby suddenly became a boomtown. But not for long. The fight promotion sacked the town.

When the chief banker of Shelby, George H. Stanton, was asked by Mayor Johnson and Loy Molumby for the second payment of $100,000 due Kearns, according to their contract with him, they learned there was no more money available.

"We haven't got the money," said Stanton. "Our expenses have been exceptionally high. We have only $1,600 on hand," he told Kearns.

The facts were shocking! Kearns, angered when told by Stanton that he, Kearns, could handle the promotion, replied, "I won't promote on my own. You fellows are the promoters. I'm a manager of the world heavyweight champion. I want the second installment of $100,000."

Slamming the door, he left the room quickly to discuss matters with Dempsey.

That evening, Stanton and his staff met privately with Kearns to try to straighten out the fiasco. Lawyers and influential businessmen were invited to attend. After prolonged discussions, it was decided to save the fight.

The following day, Kearns received $100,000 and the fight preparations again got under way. Dan Tracy, an oil man, guaranteed that the final installment would be paid on time. He declared that the interests of his city would be protected.

Two weeks later Tracy was discharged from his duties when Kearns learned that he could not raise the amount he had promised. It was after that blow that Kearns took over the promotion, which he declared was forced on him by the failure of the backers of the fight to make good.

Although Tex Rickard had a claim on Dempsey's services, he

made no attempt to prevent Kearns from handling the Shelby affair. When he learned of the difficulties the promotion was facing, Rickard attempted to salvage it by offering to take it out of Kearns' hands. Tex offered to pay Kearns and Gibbons the sum of $200,000 and $75,000, respectively.

Dempsey at this point was willing to let Tex take over. But Kearns objected, as did Gibbons, who was willing to take his chances.

It was as a result of the Shelby fiasco that the famous Rickard-Dempsey-Kearns alliance became firm. Henceforth, Dempsey cast his lot with Rickard in all promotions. This partnership put on some of the biggest extravaganzas in the history of sports.

On fight day, July 4, Dempsey had a good corps of advisors in his corner: Joe Benjamin, a top lightweight, Red Moore, Mike Trant, Trainer Jerry Luvadis, and Kearns. Gibbons was attended by Manager Eddie Kane, Trainer Papo, Bud Gorman, a heavyweight, and Jimmy Delaney, a good lightweight.

The bout finally got under way at 3:30 in the afternoon. It had been delayed because of the stalling practices of Kearns, who was keeping his eyes peeled on the box office. A crowd of only 7,202 paid $201,485. Throughout the fight, the 32-year-old Gibbons, like a coyote, kept running and twisting, but got home safely at the end of the chase. He was panting, bleeding, but safe when the final gong sounded. The bout was rather like a greyhound and hare affair.

Gibbons proved to be the best defensive fighter Dempsey had ever met. His cleverness and elusiveness saved him from being hammered to the floor by Dempsey's ever-determined attacks. Tom, at 175½ pounds—12½ lighter than Dempsey—was fast for the first ten rounds, then seemed to tire, depending almost exclusively on his superb defensive skills to take him through the final five rounds. The outcome was a complete surprise to the world of pugilism; Dempsey had been expected to stop Gibbons within ten rounds.

In the opinion of some sportswriters, had Dempsey gone all out as he did in his other battles, he could have ended the bout by a knockout. But Manassa Jack was following Kearns' orders.

On the other hand, there were those reporters who wrote that Dempsey had lost his sting and that his days as the champ were numbered. They felt that Jack had not had enough *real* fighting time, that his one hour or so of fighting time (Miske, Brennan, Carpentier) since gaining the heavyweight laurels had taken its toll.

No matter, Gibbons was mighty—and rightly—proud of his feat. It was a sad Gibbons, however, who walked out of the ring following the decision. Not because he thought he had won, but because there was nothing in the till for him to take home. His was purely a work for glory.

So discouraged were the fans that they flooded the aisles with seat cushions. Many rushed the ring to cut a slice out of the canvas for a souvenir. It was with considerable difficulty that Kearns and Dempsey made their way to the dressing room, from which, not long after, they made a hasty exit with the gate receipts.

The fact that about half the spectators in the arena were on the cuff—many having broken into the stadium without much effort—was responsible for the heavy losses sustained.

The sports world was shocked at what had happened.

The town of Shelby had been financially ruined. The Stanton Trust and Savings Bank of Great Falls had failed. Stanton's First State Bank of Shelby had been taken over by the state bank examiner to protect deposits of local residents. All bank accounts were frozen by the governing body.

"Millionaires" found themselves paupers.

Even the Silver Grill Cafe, the pride of Shelby, met its doom. Nothing was salvaged.

The story of Shelby's venture into the fight-promotion game has to rank as one of the historic events in American pugilism.

In discussing the Shelby fiasco, Dempsey told of the difficulties encountered in that promotion. Here's Jack's story:

"I was opposed to the fight because I couldn't see how the group promoting the affair could pay the $300,000 Kearns had arranged for me to obtain. I agreed to fight only on condition that I should receive $100,000 15 days prior to the affair, plus 50 percent of the picture rights.

"Despite an oil and real estate boom, the second payment was not delivered when due. So now the promoters brought the American Legion into the thing for a percentage of the profits, although the legionnaires knew there would be no profits and so did I.

"That's when I contacted Rickard, who was willing to take over and stage the fight in New York and pay the expenses already accumulated. But Kearns strenuously objected. He wanted to carry on without the aid of Rickard. The people in Montana also were opposed to shifting the fight. They insisted it must take place in their state.

"Kearns got tough with them and they came up with the second $100,000. When the final $100,000 was due, there was no more money left. I was mad at the Shelby people for having turned down Rickard's offer, and that's when Kearns and I demanded the final $100,000.

"After a couple of hours, Kearns decided to put the fight on again, with him and me handling the money at the gate. When word got out that I was going to get the gate money, the cowboys tossed lariats over the posts and pulled the gates down. Thus many people got in free.

"When it was all over, I hurried to get out of town. The financial ruin of Shelby had been completed. I ran all the way to the training center, about a mile, after the fight had been completed," Dempsey concluded.

When Gibbons was in London several months after the fight with Dempsey, a trip he made to fight Jack Bloomfield at the National Sporting Club, Colonel Eddie Eagan, then an Oxford student, helped train Tom. Eagan asked Gibbons why he was continuing in the fight game after the poor deal he received in his affair with Dempsey. Tom replied:

"One must eat. If he has a big family as I have, he must find the means to support a wife and children. That's why I accepted the offer to fight Bloomfield. There must be a better way to care for your family," he told Eagan.

"As you know, I fought Dempsey on a percentage basis. Well, he got virtually every penny that came in at the gate to make up his $300,000 contract. I took a chance on a percentage and got nothing, or virtually nothing, in addition to losing the money I brought with me for expenses and training partners.

"The bank in Shelby, as you know, went broke. The money I had deposited in that bank was lost through its failure and all I got out of the mess were Dempsey's punches and a flattened pocketbook. But I did manage to get a vaudeville contract. Though it didn't amount to much, it did help me a little. I had to compete with trained seals to get enough money to feed the wife and kids."

19

Watching Dempsey wrest the world heavyweight title from Willard, I wondered how the victim could stand such punishment.

Seeing Joe Louis, out to avenge his earlier humiliating defeat, tear into Max Schmeling in the opening round of their return battle, gave me a thrill such as I had seldom experienced while attending a fistic engagement.

But I must confess that the highlight of such experiences in a period of more than threescore years of sports reporting was the Dempsey–Luis Angel (Wild Bull of the Pampas) Firpo fight on September 14, 1923, at the Polo Grounds in New York City. It was the night that Dempsey knocked out his strong adversary in the second round of a contest in which the Argentinian punched Manassa Jack out of the ring in the opening round.

It was an occasion when the South American had the world heavyweight title within grasp but was unable to tighten his grip on it. For thrills, one finds it most difficult to select a heavyweight championship match that carried more enduring memories.

When the Wild Bull of the Pampas made his appearance against Dempsey, a gathering of 82,000 persons, who paid $1,-188,603 to see the action, honored him with acclaim fit for a king. An historical gathering it was too, for this was the first of Rickard's promotions staged at night, and a most successful one from any angle one chooses to view it.

Firpo had come to the United States at the invitation of Rickard, who had discovered him in Argentina. Tex realized that opponents for Dempsey were scarce. He figured that a big brawny foreigner would draw another huge gate, like the one Carpentier had drawn when he fought Manassa Jack. Rickard banked on the general appearance of the Argentinian—more so than on Luis's fighting qualifications—to accomplish this feat.

That Tex was correct was proven when the final tally was made. Rickard, a man of great vision, thus far had not erred in any of his ventures. His knowledge of the fight-promotion field and the sports public was unexcelled.

Firpo was virtually unknown in the United States. He had engaged in 15 fights in South America, a few of which Rickard had seen. Tex hoped that because of the Argentinian's fierce appearance and the large number of South American and other Spanish-speaking sports fans in the States, especially in New York, he could build the fighter into a top attraction. His plan worked exceedingly well.

Firpo refused to pose for pictures. He turned down requests for interviews and otherwise turned into an obnoxious character insofar as reporters were concerned.

Normally the attitude assumed by the Argentinian would be regarded as detrimental to the buildup of a million-dollar sports event. However, in this case, the elements involved were different from those usually encountered. And Tex was successful in exploiting this negative attitude.

Firpo not only shunned interviews but also insisted on being paid for his appearances at training sessions, which fact irked Rickard. Since the promoter could speak Spanish and was held in high regard in South American countries, he finally convinced Firpo that things weren't done that way in our country. By putting aside some extra spending money for him, Tex placed the big, husky pugilist on firmer financial ground.

For further protection, Rickard appointed a Spanish interpreter, who was highly esteemed by members of the Argentinian embassy, thus helping to get the fighter down to Mother Earth. Firpo agreed to the new arrangements. Now Rickard got busy on further plans for Luis's buildup.

A number of heavyweights were in New York at the time and the promoter decided to make use of them in the buildup matches. Newark, N.J., was the scene for the first appearance of the bulky South American. A bout was arranged with Tom Maxted, a tough heavyweight. Firpo put him away in the seventh round. Next came a bout with Joe McCann. He was stopped in the sixth canto. Then followed a bout with a bulky Italian from Brooklyn, Jack Herman. He was disposed of by Luis in the fifth frame.

Firpo became restless. With plenty of money in his jeans, he grew homesick. He told Rickard he wanted to return to Argentina to purchase cattle. Tex had no objection.

In the meantime, a bout had been arranged with Jim Tracey for Buenos Aires. Firpo put his opponent away in the fourth round. It was all part of the excellent buildup. For each bout, the attendance was large. The fact that Firpo was under contract to an American promoter added to Luis's popularity at home.

When Rickard was ready for Firpo's New York campaign, he had Luis return to the States. On his arrival, the promoter decided to pit the fighter against a few tough opponents in the final buildup. Bouts with Bill Brennan and Jack McAuliffe were arranged. Brennan was stopped in the 12th round and McAuliffe in the third.

In Havana, Firpo put Jack Herman away in the second round. Then followed a knockout of Jim Hibbard in Mexico in the second round. In Jersey City, July 1923, Firpo stopped ex-champ Willard in the eighth round. Joe Burke was next. He went out in the second, Charley Weinert, a rough one, became the final victim. He went out in the second round in Philadelphia.

The Argentinian had now become an outstanding attraction. No longer did Rickard have to worry about Luis and the public. The buildup of Tex's importation was now complete. In each of his contests the Argentinian had given proof that, although he knew little about the finer points of boxing; lacked finesse; clubbed instead of throwing punches according to Hoyle; he was a tough, vicious, and very formidable fighter. He was now ready for the purpose Rickard had in mind.

Rickard was now certain he could pit Firpo against Dempsey with the wholehearted support of the boxing-minded public. The Wild Bull of the Pampas had proved his value both as a drawing card and as a suitable opponent for the world champion.

Thus, on September 14, 1923, one of the most spectacular heavyweight fights of all time took place before 82,000 wild-eyed spectators. Though only an inch and a half shorter than the Wild Bull, Dempsey looked much smaller. His 192½ pounds when measured against Firpo's 216½ pounds gave him the appearance of meagerness. Many of the fans were awed by the Argentinian's bulk. But pounds were not the decisive issue in this contest, which featured 11 knockdowns. Except for the punch that landed Manassa Jack into the laps of several newsmen, the battle belonged to Dempsey.

The challenger was floored seven times in the opening round and twice in the second before being counted out. Within the three minutes and 57 seconds of terrific milling, Dempsey was knocked out of the ring in the first frame. Were it not for the friendly hands of members of the working press, he might have been counted out himself. Within the first ten seconds of the bout, Jack was put on his knees but jumped up without a count.

Firpo failed to follow up the advantage he had gained late in the opening round when he knocked Manassa Jack out of the ring. He achieved that feat seemingly with superhuman strength *after* having visited the canvas on seven occasions.

It was a case of a primitive man, a wild beast of the South American jungle, pitting mere strength against the know-how of a champion with all the tricks of the trade at his command. Firpo soon became aware that strength alone couldn't win for him against a well-trained fighter whose scowl was enough to scare the average pugilist half to death.

The unexpected had happened in the opening round, but the ferociousness of the tiger facing Firpo in the second turned the tide and enabled Dempsey to keep the world crown in the United States.

A few seconds after the bell clanged for the first round, Firpo landed a ponderous right to Dempsey's jaw, dropping the champ to his knees. More off balance than hurt, Dempsey leaped up without a count.

Dempsey then advanced upon his prey, landing a cobralike left hook to the Argentinian's jaw, flooring him. Like Jack, Firpo bounced up without a count. After a looping right caught Dempsey on the jaw but failed to faze him, Dempsey sent a left uppercut to Luis's chin, sending him to his knees. As Firpo struggled to his feet, Dempsey, who had been standing over him, connected with a left and a right. Another left hook to the chin floored the South American again.

When Firpo pulled himself erect, Dempsey, hovering over him, dropped Luis with a right to the head, his fourth trip downward. A few seconds later, Firpo thudded to the canvas for the fifth time, thanks to a left and right combination from Dempsey. As soon as Firpo arose, Dempsey connected with a vicious right, Luis again going down. The gritty, game South American dragged himself to his feet at nine, only to run into another left and right, which sent him down for the seventh time. Somehow, he managed to get up just before Referee Johnny Gallagher reached the ten count.

By dint of a marvelous reserve of strength, Firpo then bulled Dempsey across the ring, forcing him to the ropes. Then, winding up like a baseball pitcher, Firpo landed a long overhand right to the head, sending the champion through the ropes, across the apron, and into the working-press section as the crowd roared. The sight of Dempsey being pushed back into the ring, the savagery with which he had been hurtled through the ropes into the laps of reporters, the wild-eyed spectators standing, leaping into the air, shouting encouragement to their respective favorite, was something the like of which I had never experienced in all my years of witnessing famous ring battles.

The momentary agony of Dempsey's supporters turned into a state of bedlam as Jack was pushed back into the ring by friendly hands, contrary to the rules of boxing.

Everyone in the ballpark was in a frenzy as Dempsey returned to the ring. Moments later came the clang of the gong ending that thrilling, never-to-be-forgotten opening round.

During the minute rest period, the seconds worked feverishly in Dempsey's corner while most of the spectators stood and cheered—women and men alike. It was an emotional scene such as seldom before had been witnessed in a New York arena.

A tense Dempsey, rarin' to go, eager to leap at his foe, his gloved hands moving to and fro, awaited the gong for the second round.

Scarce had it clanged than Dempsey leaped out of his stool toward Firpo. The Wild Bull, with a strange look, eyed the champion, indicating he hadn't expected such a quick movement from a foe who, minutes before, had been on the brink of disaster. The bulldog tenacity for which Dempsey has been admired was now in evidence. Thousands of his supporters cheered as Jack lashed at his opponent with lefts and rights.

The recuperative powers of the champion evoked praise from the writers at ringside. The killer was now after his prey. He had been humiliated in the first round and now he was prepared to make his opponent pay in full.

Firpo, urged on by his chief second, raised his right over his head, preparing to crash it on his opponent. But Dempsey, calling on all his reserve power, stepped in and drove a powerful left to the body. The South American giant dropped his hands and gasped for breath. Like a giant oak following the crash of the woodsman's axe, Firpo swayed and tumbled to the canvas.

Now behind him, now in front, now to one side, then the other, ever prepared to deliver the coup-de-grace the moment Firpo got to his feet, moved Dempsey, never taking his eyes off his wounded victim.

Luis got to his feet. After a short exchange, Dempsey once more drove a powerful left to Firpo's stomach. A right to the jaw immediately followed. Firpo fell forward on his face. Blood was streaming from several wounds.

Firpo's lips were split and his face began to puff. The referee, amidst wild shouts from the vast gathering, counted the doleful decimal over the visitor from Argentina. The most furious battle on record was over. As the tenth stroke of the referee's count was completed, Firpo tried to rise, but couldn't.

With the fight over, there followed the pushing and shoving of those eager to reach ringside, a mad rush of the writers to the dressing room to obtain interviews, a throng of spectators tugging and shoving, all clamoring for a chance to take a look at the champion.

What a scene!

The most dramatic part of the contest was the scene following Dempsey's being knocked through the ropes and the excitement of Referee Gallagher as he stood bewildered, now knowing whether to start the count that might send the title to South America, or to wait for Dempsey to return to the ring. Gallagher explained his indecision by stating he wasn't certain whether the champion was pushed or was sent out of the ring by a punch. No matter what his thoughts were, the thousands who witnessed the fight were certain they had seen Manassa Jack struck by a blow that hurtled him into the laps of several world-famous newsmen.

Had Firpo's brain power approached his strength, he would have been crowned heavyweight king that night. With all the power at his command, the strength to give and take punishment, he lacked one essential—a fighting brain. He had the world's richest title within his grasp, but let the opportunity slip away. The wild-eyed, infuriated giant from Argentina saw his opponent swaying groggily before him after his return from outside the ring, but the Wild Bull was unequal to the task at hand.

Dempsey, on the other hand, displayed all the assets of a fighting fury, gathering all his resources in the second round and using them to full advantage.

In this battle, Dempsey committed several fouls for which he was not penalized because of the wild excitement of the huge throng and the laxity of Referee Gallagher. First, the referee didn't count over Dempsey, who was being aided by newspapermen, after being knocked out of the ring. Second, the official did not pay proper attention to the count after Manassa Jack had been pushed back into the ring. Dempsey may have received a much longer count, had it been recorded, than did Tunney in his Chicago bout with Manassa Jack.

It was the Firpo fight that brought about changes in the boxing rules in New York, rules which have since been in force in every part of the world. One change required that a boxer who has scored a knockdown retire to a neutral corner. He must remain in that corner to await the signal of the referee before he can resume fighting.

An odd incident occurred in the fight at the end of the opening round. Kearns was hunting for the smelling salts to aid Dempsey, but couldn't locate the bottle. All afoam, Kearns shouted to his aides—to no avail. Through all the excitement Kearns had had the smelling salts in his pocket.

The only calm person in the corner between rounds was Dempsey. He turned to Joe Benjamin, one of his seconds, and asked for the water bottle. Then, noting the buzz, he remarked, "What's all this about? Why all the excitement?"

20

THE CELEBRATION of Jack Dempsey's 75th birthday, June 24, 1970, as on many other occasions since he retired, brought forth many news items about his career, including his close association with Jack Kearns. A comparison of the champion with former heavyweight kings, his rise to fistic fame during the Golden Era of Boxing, the part both Rickard and Kearns had in his rise to the world crown—these and other items were discussed on the occasion.

One subject which attracted my attention was that which pertained to the failure of Dempsey to fight Harry Wills. In an article appearing in a New York paper, the writer stated that Dempsey, like the great John L. Sullivan, steered clear of Negro opponents and that Jack could not be persuaded to enter the ring in combat with Wills, the New Orleans Brown Panther.

Neither is a correct statement. I was close to that story from its beginning and am aware of all the details of the false charge. During the first few weeks in New York when Dempsey was making his Eastern debut, he accepted three fights, one of which was with John Lester Johnson, a burly, tough Negro whom he faced in the Harlem Sporting Club. It was a ten-round no-decision affair, due to the law at the time.

Thereafter, there were many more Negroes on the list of his opponents. On two occasions he came close to fighting Harry Wills. That he didn't wasn't his fault.

When Rickard attempted to pit Jack against Harry in Yankee Stadium, Tex was warned by politicians to lay off. To show his good faith, after he had been lambasted for so-called discrimination against the Negro race, Rickard got Paddy Mullins, manager of Wills, to agree to have Harry and Dempsey fight in Jersey City. That such a match was actually made is evident by the fact that I have a ticket showing a bout set for Saturday, November 8, 1924.

Rickard, after consulting members of the governor's staff and other top officials, learned that the risk was too great. They were opposed to having a mixed heavyweight championship match staged for fear of race riots, and so informed Tex.

John Ringling and Mike Jacobs, partner and advisor, respectively, of Rickard, also were told the same thing. New Jersey's higher-ups had informed Rickard's advisors that such a bout would not be permitted in that state. That is why Rickard abandoned further consideration of the match.

Let's examine the record of the Wills-Dempsey controversy.

Starting in 1922, court injunctions and boxing commission edicts had been issued against Dempsey as a result of pleas for recognition by Wills. Finally, to calm Harry, Rickard's ingenuity came to the rescue. An agreement was entered into between Wills and Dempsey.

On July 11, 1922, a contract was signed. It stipulated that the date be set within 60 days after a reliable promoter undertook to stage the bout. The articles signed merely indicated good faith on the part of the boxers to come together in ring combat. Three important issues were ignored—the place, date, and terms.

Paddy Mullins, noting that all was not straightforward, insisted that Kearns accept an agreement to have all bids submitted within 30 days, including two other changes forced upon him —that neither Wills nor Dempsey could engage in another bout during the terms of the contract, and that if a Dempsey-Wills bout were to be staged in New York, the rules of the commission must be in effect.

The New York Commission also insisted that Dempsey must sign for a Wills bout, no matter where it was to be staged, or Jack would lose his boxing license. To add to the confusion, the New York Commission declared that the fight, if staged, could not be held in New York State.

"What an enigma! A Chinese puzzle," the press stated. Indeed it was! It was a most laughable situation, so much so that the New York Commission was ridiculed in many newspapers throughout the country.

One of the stories that continue to survive is that Dempsey wanted no part of Wills and that he and Kearns, with Rickard's connivance, did all in their power to confuse the public so as to make the match impossible.

Discussing that aspect with Dempsey recently, he told me:

"You know that is false. You were with Kearns, Bob Edgren, Vincent Treanor, Jimmy Dawson of the *New York Times,* and me in the office of Rickard at the time he had arranged to stage the fight in Jersey City, when Tex, after a dispute with Mullins, Wills' manager, turned to Kearns and said, 'The fight cannot be held in Jersey City. I just spoke to Frank Hague, the Democratic boss of Jersey City, and he told me the governor won't stand for it. I'm now going to get another opponent for an outdoor show. We'll forget Wills.'

"That's the true reason why I never fought Wills. To stop Mullins from complaining and to stop unwarranted attacks against me by the press, I had accepted the proposition of Floyd Fitzsimmons to fight Wills in Michigan but when the time came for Floyd to put up my portion of the guarantee, he told Kearns he didn't have the money. He said he gave Mullins $50,000 for Wills' share and couldn't raise any more. That's why the fight never took place.

"I've been accused of discrimination against Wills because he was black. Any promoter who could or would have put up the money for my end of the purse could have had the fight. But no one came forth.

"If you recall, William Muldoon, a member of the boxing commission, called a meeting of the press and told reporters that while he definitely wanted a Wills-Dempsey match, so long as he was a member of the commission, there would be no heavyweight championship mixed match in New York. Yet he insisted that I sign for such a fight. How ridiculous!

"Here is a clipping from your paper, the *New York Press.* Your writer, George B. Underwood, expresses himself as being satisfied that I was sincere and honest in my declarations of readiness to fight Wills. He was a top Wills supporter, as you know.

"Rickard received a message from State Senator James J. Walker in which the legislator told him that if the mixed bout were staged in New York, it would bring about the repeal of the Walker Law. That's why Rickard abandoned it, I was told by Walker."

When the Firpo-Dempsey match was announced in 1923, Mullins became indignant. He started court action. Three days before the Dempsey-Firpo fight, he tried to get a mandamus to stop that bout and to substitute Wills for Firpo, but Justice Hagerty of Brooklyn, before whom the writ was argued, refused to act on it favorably.

In a lengthy opinion, the jurist declared that the State Athletic Commission had no authority to order the Dempsey-Wills bout to take place, before a time, place, and promoter had been agreed upon for such a contest. He therefore denied the motion. The victory came as a jolt to those who wanted to prevent Dempsey from fighting.

Muldoon, following the application of Wills for the mandamus, declared that no boxer could force the hands of the New York Commission to act contrary to its best judgment. He said he was certain no court would overrule the act of the State Athletic Commission, a body empowered by the law to carry on boxing according to the rules and regulations laid down by that body. He said he granted a license for the Dempsey-Firpo bout because he was opposed to a Dempsey-Wills contest.

21

IT WASN'T LONG after Dempsey had become heavyweight champion that he was urged to make stage appearances and enter the movies. Actually Jack didn't like that kind of life. He quickly learned that acting was not one of his major assets. People came to see him, not for his histrionic ability, of course, but for his personality and fighting qualities. Nevertheless, he did enter show business and went to Hollywood, where he received $1,000 a week from Pathé. He never earned less than that and often made more.

He quickly became good friends with such stars as Charlie Chaplin, Douglas Fairbanks, Sr., and Wallace Reid.

For the next several years, Jack was in and out of movie town. In the main, his movie career consisted of a film called *Manhattan Madness* with Estelle Taylor and two serials—*Daredevil Jack* and *Fight and Win.* Dempsey was also under contract to Carl Laemmle, head of Universal Pictures for several years.

In the rip-roaring *Daredevil Jack,* he wasn't much of an actor, but the picture went over well. The public liked it and it did good business. Dempsey and Kearns split large royalties on it for almost seven years. Everytime Manassa Jack was billed for a fight, the film received another airing.

Dempsey also completed a two-reeler, *Win, Lose or Draw,* at Warner Brothers' Vitaphone Studio in Brooklyn. In it, he let fly many hooks at his opponents. Dempsey, striving for realism, put plenty of vim behind his punches, particularly the damaging left hooks with which he knocked out his opponents.

Jack's supporting cast included Zulu Kid, Eddie Roberts, King Solomon, Bob Savage, Babe Herman, and Irish Tommy Jordan. The golden-throated Joe Humphreys had charge of the ring microphone and Sam Taub, of *The Ring,* called the punches, in his usual rapid-fire style, into a dummy microphone at ringside.

In one of the Hollywood serials, the director, Erle Kenton, wanted to use a double for Jack in a scene where the champion was supposed to stop a runaway team of horses. When Dempsey found out about the double, he hitched up his belt a couple of notches and declared,

"Bring on the ponies, I'm all ready for them."

"Not you, Jack," said Kenton. "We've got an experienced horseman ready to double for you."

But Dempsey stood his ground. He insisted on playing his own scenes. The results proved highly satisfactory to all concerned. Dempsey displayed a burst of speed that would have done credit to Charlie Paddock, the Fastest Human of the day, by stopping the team of horses without even losing his derby hat.

The highlight of Jack's stage career was a play called *The Big Fight,* in which he starred with his wife, Estelle Taylor, on Broadway. Jack received $1,000 a week and Miss Taylor $300.

In the play, Dempsey was cast as "The Tiger." The drama was built around a fight camp where crookedness abounded among the hangers-on. The action ran through intrigue, love, heroism, and the double-cross. The climax occurred when "The Tiger" defended his title, good name, and honor against Battling Baker, "The Pride of the Far East," whom Dempsey knocked out in the second round.

In the final stages, "The Tiger" rose to dramatic heights as he stalked and clawed his prey.

Corny? The utmost!

But there was stark realism in Jack's left hook and a right cross that carried a hefty wallop. Jack's footwork could have been better, but it was good enough, judging by the applause his performance received.

As for Dempsey's speech and gestures, Jack admitted he couldn't act, but once the bell clanged for action, the spectators were well treated. They saw what they had paid to witness—real action.

The Big Fight touched on the Estelle Taylor–Dempsey romance. Several lines in the play clearly pointed to the break between Dempsey and Kearns over La Belle Estelle.

"Why you bum, so you're quitting me now" is an illustration. "I picked you up out of the gutter and made a world champion out of you," said the Kearnslike character.

At one stage, Dempsey was asked to throw the manager out of a barbershop where they were arguing. Dempsey performed the feat, but against his wishes. Dempsey was irritated, indicating a revulsion for the scene. But he did it with "grace and ease." The spectators, acquainted with the Kearns-Dempsey situation, jeered. It was too mild a performance.

The producers likewise were uneasy. They figured that Dempsey should have performed the act with vigor and ferocity in ejecting the man with whom he now was at odds.

Most of the spectators went to the show in order to see what Dempsey could do with a speaking part and left with the realization that as an actor, Dempsey was a flop. Only when he tossed punches did he arouse enthusiasm.

The play revolved around a sure-thing gambler, who tried to put the championship in the bag, and when Dempsey protested, the spectators cheered.

"I always fight to win," snapped Jack. "I don't cheat."

The house came down with a roar.

At the termination of the second act, the stage was flooded with floral tributes from Dempsey's friends and the management.

David Belasco, famed theatrical producer who directed the affair, was asked to comment on Jack's acting. Replied Belasco:

"This is a man with the strength of Samson, but at heart he is a great big boy."

Through the cheering, Dempsey and Estelle stood on the stage smiling. Dempsey then walked to the center, held up his hands for silence, and addressed the house:

"Ladies and Gentlemen. This is tougher than any round I ever had to fight."

The reference was not to the show but to the ordeal. As the play ended following the flattening of his opponent, Dempsey said:

"I'm through with the whole mess."

Among those champions who performed in the movies the first was Jess Willard. He was in a picture called *A Fighting Chance.* He did a good job. In the feature, he bowled over about thirty rowdies in a free-for-all, each one being disposed of with a single blow. On one occasion the director wasn't satisfied with the action and ordered it refilmed. Many of those in the free-for-all scene objected to being the victim of another knockout blow, but the scene was refilmed and the picture made a hit with the public.

A Fighting Chance was released about ten days before the Willard-Dempsey fight. Ironically, it was shown in Toledo theaters on the day of the bout. After the annihilation of Jess, it was removed.

Following the knockout, one of the newsmen covering the affair unthoughtfully yelled to Willard as Jess was sitting in his corner:

"Jess, why didn't you save some of those punches you used in the movie for Dempsey? You could have used them."

Gene Tunney, following Dempsey, made a picture, but it was never released. Max Schmeling was a hit in Germany in the film *Love in the Ring,* for which he received a down payment of $50,000 plus royalties, the largest sum paid to any boxer.

Dempsey, who had been divorced from Maxine Cates before the Fulton fight in 1918, married film star Estelle Taylor on February 7, 1925. Jack Kearns didn't like her and the feeling was mutual. It marked the beginning of the end of the successful fighter-pilot combo.

There had been some previous disputes between Dempsey and Kearns over money and one incident after another caused the rift to widen even further.

Estelle never cared much for Jack's way of earning a living. After watching him training for his return match with Tunney in 1927, she told reporters:

"It's revolting. I wouldn't go to see Jack sock Tunney down in their big fight for anything. There's big money in this prize-fighting for us, but the money doesn't get any bigger because I watch it."

She stayed in her Chicago hotel room on the night of the "long count," but collapsed when she heard the radio announcement of Dempsey's defeat.

Jack divorced her in Reno in 1931 on grounds of mental cruelty. The suit was uncontested. In 1943, Estelle married Paul Small, motion picture producer and agent. They were divorced two years later. Estelle died in 1958 at the age of 58, of cancer. Dempsey was her second husband.

She had appeared in such hit films as *Cimarron, Street Scene, The Southerner,* and Cecil B. DeMille's early version of *The Ten Commandments.*

Luis Angel (Wild Bull of the Pampas) Firpo himself. The Argentinian was stopped by Dempsey in two rounds in what was perhaps the wildest ring battle ever seen.

Dempsey is knocked into the press row by Firpo in the first round of their unforgettable battle at New York's Polo Grounds on September 14, 1923. Manassa Jack came back to KO the Wild Bull in the next round.

From left, Jess McMahon, Tex Rickard, Jimmy DeForest, Dempsey, and Estelle Taylor. Photo was snapped on the liner *Berengaria.*

Rickard discusses a few things with Dempsey upon the latter's arrival in New York for bout with Jack Sharkey in July 1927. Nontitle contest drew over a million dollars. Dempsey scored a seventh-round KO.

Dempsey displays physique to the crowd attending a training session as Jack prepared for his return match with Gene Tunney.

Tunney listens intently as Referee Dave Barry intones the famed "long count" in the seventh round of the historic second Tunney-Dempsey meeting in Chicago on September 22, 1927. Gene arose at nine, but many experts maintain he was on the floor anywhere from 14 to 18 seconds.

Jack smiles approval as his father plays a tune on the violin.

Dempsey in an affectionate pose with his mother in 1929.

22

By the time 1926 rolled around, Dempsey and Kearns had split openly. The manager had done a few things with Jack's money that the Manassa Mauler didn't like. Dempsey told him the only way he could remain with him was to accept a 33 percent cut instead of the 50 percent he had been taking. Besides, he owed Dempsey a lot of money.

Kearns refused to go along with the new deal and told Dempsey, "You'll never fight again."

In March 1926 Kearns sued Dempsey, claiming breach of contract. After a trial marked by much bitterness, Kearns lost. He kept on with a series of suits, however, that lasted for several years.

At any rate, Dempsey hadn't fought in a contest for almost three years. The New York State Athletic Commission, still pressed by Manager Paddy Mullins for a match between Dempsey and Harry Wills, took up the issue with Rickard.

Rickard had shunted the Negro heavyweight to the sidelines,

insisting that officials in the state capital Albany were opposed to a mixed match.

Tex remained adamant in the matter. He told Mullins and the commission that such a bout would be against the public interest.

Rickard, instead, wanted Dempsey to face Gene Tunney, conqueror of Tom Gibbons and Georges Carpentier, in New York. Dempsey, who by this time had engaged Gene Normile as his manager, agreed to the contest. Jack actually was his own boss, however; Normile attended only to business details.

When the New York Commission refused to sanction a Dempsey-Tunney bout in New York, saying that Dempsey had to meet Wills or nobody, Rickard turned to Philadelphia for the championship heavyweight contest.

Tex had been informed by Quaker City officials that the gigantic Sesquicentennial Stadium was available for such a match. Rickard, after several secret meetings with the Philadelphia moguls, told New York Commissioners William Muldoon, James A. Farley, and George Brower that Tunney was his choice to face Dempsey, not Wills, and that if the commission failed to change its collective mind and sanction the bout, he would take the Dempsey-Tunney bout elsewhere.

Farley and Brower still insisted that Dempsey must face Wills before any other contender. As for Muldoon, though he also agreed that Wills should be Dempsey's next opponent, he did not want a mixed match in New York, fearing a race riot, whatever the outcome.

Paddy Mullins decided to take the issue to the courts, but met with a setback. Through the efforts of Commissioners Farley and Brower, strong supporters of Wills, Dempsey was banned from fighting in New York until he had given Harry a shot at the title.

At a conference in his office, Rickard informed the press that he had gone as far as he could to satisfy the whims of the commission, but found it a hopeless task. "I've decided," he said, "to take the Dempsey-Tunney fight to Philadelphia where there will be no interference. I have the support of the Pennsylvania Boxing Commission."

That Rickard's choice was an excellent one was proven by the huge turnout (120,757) for the fight and by the gate receipts of $1,895,733, each a record at the time. The latter, however, would stand for only a year, until the return engagement between Gene and Jack in Chicago in 1927, when official receipts would tally over two and a half million dollars.

How did Rickard get Tunney into the championship picture?

Tunney, as the American light heavyweight king, was eager to fight in the top division. In his quest for higher honors, Gene had fought and beaten Martin Burke, and knocked out Erminio Spalla, Carpentier, Gibbons, Italian Jack Herman, and Bartley Madden. Rickard believed Gene was now ready to engage Dempsey.

Except for a few exhibition bouts, Jack had been idle since knocking out Firpo. He now wanted action and requested Rickard to obtain a match for him. Tex had immediately realized that Tunney's feat in stopping Gibbons in 12 was not to be taken lightly. It topped the 15-round decision Dempsey had gained over Tom, so Rickard decided to strike while the iron was hot. He set into motion negotiations with Tunney for a fight with the champion.

After the promoter received Dempsey's okay to negotiate, Tex sent a telegram to Tunney asking for a meeting in New York City the following day. Tunney consented.

Tunney's friend, Bill McCabe, whom Gene had met in France, was brought into the negotiations. Bill was to arrange for a meeting place suitable for the occasion.

"I told McCabe," said Tex, "that Dempsey had requested me to get Gene as his next opponent in a title match."

When Tunney and McCabe appeared the following day, Rickard objected to the meeting place chosen. He told Gene that he wanted more privacy than that which McCabe had provided.

"We don't want to be seen here," cautioned Tex. "The place is wide open. Let's have more privacy."

The trio then went to the opposite side of the street where the home of Gene's friend, Jimmy Eagleton, was situated.

Although Rickard found Tunny a willing listener, he wasn't absolutely certain Gene really wanted to fight the Manassa Mauler. He asked Gene if he could bank on his word that he, Tunney, would go through with the bout if Tex could reach an agreement with both him and Dempsey.

"I've been waiting for this chance," assured Gene. "You can

count on me. It's the fight I've been thinking about for a long time."

That was all Rickard wanted to know. The match was clinched. He and Gene shook hands as a binder. Arrangements were completed for the principals and their legal representatives to meet Rickard the following day to sign the contract and to arrange the details.

The date for the bout was September 23, 1926.

As previously promised, Quaker City officials turned over to Rickard the use of Sesquicentennial Stadium, with its huge seating capacity of over 120,000. Rickard was confident the bout would be a tremendous moneymaker. Again his foresight proved infallible.

Rickard and his aides quickly got busy arranging the undercard. Training camps were acquired, and the preliminaries for another million-dollar gate got under way, this time with Kearns out of the picture.

Dempsey set up his training camp in Atlantic City, New Jersey. There he found it necessary to have his surroundings fortified with barbed wire to protect himself and his entourage from being molested by private detectives who had surrounded the Dempsey quarters. Hired by Kearns, they tried to serve Manassa Jack with legal papers and put their hands on anything of value belonging to him.

Process servers stopped Estelle Taylor, Jack's wife, as she was driving out of the grounds, and handed her a writ. They confiscated the car given her two days before by her husband. It was a trying time for the world champion and definitely impeded his training.

Tunney established his camp at Stroudsburg, Pennsylvania, where he had the privacy he sought.

23

Unlike Joe Louis in later days, Dempsey failed to live up to his original declaration when he won the title, that he would be a fighting champion. He defended the crown only six times in a period of seven years. The stage and movies took up much of his time. And when he was not before the spotlight, he was engaged in boxing exhibitions or was with a circus. He became ring-rusty. His managerial difficulties also had taken their toll. When the time came to confront Tunney, he was far different from the Dempsey who had worked his way up the pugilistic ladder.

Dempsey, now 31, was about to face a determined 29-year-old New Yorker who, in addition to being a clever mitt artist, had maintained himself in the top conditioning he had received while with the marines during World War I. Dempsey, throughout his training period in Atlantic City, had been struck far more often by sparmates then he had been while tuning up for his previous bouts.

When September 23 came, Jack's spirit was there but his

flesh was not wholly cooperative. The story of the Philadelphia affair may aptly be titled, "The Punch That Failed."

In the Quaker City battle, Manassa Jack, like many of his predecessors among the great champions of the past, joined the ranks of those who had found a long layoff costly. The flame in his fighting heart was now barely flickering. The singlemindedness that once was his own brand eluded him. Legal matters, business affairs, Estelle—these competed for his attention, and helped to grease the skids for his downfall.

On the day of the fight, I was one of the reporters permitted by the Pennsylvania Commission to attend the medical examination of Tunney in the executive offices of Commissioner Frank Weiner. Tunney extended his hand in greeting both to me and to his friend, Jimmy Dawson, sportswriter of the *New York Times.* Gene's hand was cold. Dawson was the first to remark it.

Tunney, weighing 192—two pounds heavier than Dempsey—went into the ring an underdog, but it soon became obvious that he, not Jack, should have been listed as the favorite.

The affair was fought in a driving rain that drenched the contestants and the 120,000-plus spectators.

That the defending titleholder had lost his punch was a fact not long hidden. With the exception of two rounds, Gene was the master. Several times he made Jack look foolish with misses. In addition to not having his old punch, Dempsey's superb defensive ability and viciousness—in fact, most of the assets which had made him so formidable a fighter in earlier days—were missing.

In four of the rounds, Dempsey started with vim, but soon petered out. The Manassa Mauler wasn't mauling anybody tonight.

Bill Brady, the man who had managed Jim Corbett and Jim Jeffries, was sitting near me. He told me that Tunney reminded him of Corbett when Gentleman Jim fought John L. Sullivan. "This is very much a duplicate of that fight. Gene will win this one. He's too good for Jack."

Following is a blow-by-blow description of the fight:

Round One. Dempsey, with a scowl, rushed forth as the bell clanged. He forced Gene into the ropes. Jack let go a perfect right that landed on Gene's cheek. Dempsey kept rushing until Gene caught him with a snappy right to the chin.

As Dempsey advanced, Gene crashed a right to his jaw. After a short exchange, Gene rushed in, let go two rights, each of which caught Jack on the body. Dempsey crashed a right under the heart as the bell clanged. Dempsey walked wearily to his corner.

Round Two. As the bell clanged, Dempsey rushed out of his corner and swung a right that landed on Gene's jaw. They stepped into the center of the ring and Tunney swung a right, then a left, each of which landed perfectly. Jack drove Gene to his corner with a perfect right to the jaw. Jack continued his assault, landing with both hands and sending Gene under cover in his own corner.

They wrestled across the ring, with Dempsey's body punches checked by Gene's perfect defense. Jack then drove Gene into his corner with a perfect right under the heart. Tunney landed a solid right to Jack's jaw as the bell ended the round.

Round Three. Dempsey came out of his corner slowly. The boxers met in the center of the ring where Jack sent a right to the jaw, but the punch missed. Gene retaliated with a perfect right to the chin, then belted Jack with several blows to the jaw. Gene had Jack staggering from a right that landed with force on the chin.

As Jack came forward, Gene leaped out of his way and sparred cleverly. Dempsey attempted to connect with several rights to Jack's chin.

Round Four. Dempsey came forth with a rush and shot a right for Gene's chin but it missed. Another right caught Gene's forehead and Tunney whimpered. Another, and Gene was against the ropes. Dempsey missed a left for the jaw and Gene tagged him with a left, then a right to the chin.

A solid whack caused blood to flow from Jack's left eye. Tunney came forth with a rush. He swung a heavy right to Jack's jaw. Two rights to the jaw followed and Dempsey appeared to be hurt. They left Jack in a bad way.

A fusillade of rights and lefts followed as Tunney took advantage of the situation and Dempsey was sent back on his heels toward the ropes. Before the bell sounded, Jack rushed in and tossed several punches, two of which landed with force on Gene's cheek.

Round Five. When the bell clanged, a weary Dempsey faced Gene. They boxed in the center of the ring, following which

Gene crashed a power right to Jack's body and a left to his jaw.

Dempsey's left eye was beginning to close. He kept circling around Gene in an attempt to ward off the attacks to his head and succeeded in working Gene into a corner where Jack bombarded him with body blows.

Heavy lefts and rights to the body didn't check Tunney, who rallied quickly and sent Jack reeling back with two lefts to the body and a right to the chin. Jack then worked Gene into a neutral corner where he socked the challenger with body punches.

Again Gene rallied. Several hard body blows forced Dempsey to seek shelter. Jack let go a left for Gene's jaw but it missed and Gene's counter blow, a right to the jaw, sent Jack back on his heels. Dempsey had slowed considerably.

Round Six. Dempsey came out slowly as the bell clanged. He followed Gene to a neutral corner where Jack clinched. Gene let go several rights, each of which struck Jack's jaw. They now fought in the middle of the ring, with Gene having the better of the exchanges. A heavy left to Gene's body staggered the challenger.

Gene quickly came back with three rights to the jaw and a left to the body that staggered Jack. There was no letup in the exchanges as Dempsey retaliated with two authoritative rights to the jaw that staggered Gene. He kept crowding Tunney, who forced Dempsey toward his corner with a heavy body attack. The bell found Jack a fatigued champion.

Round Seven. Jack came out in a crouch. As he neared Gene, he let go his right, but missed the target. Jack followed with two swings for the jaw, but they didn't land with any force. Gene rushed into a clinch and Dempsey wrestled him, getting him against the ropes.

Tunney staggered the champion with a right to the jaw, following which the challenger received several hard blows in an exchange. A heavy right to the jaw staggered Dempsey.

Jack crouched, then let go a powerful right that caught Gene on the chin. Gene rushed in and followed with a right to the jaw and a left to the body.

In a heavy exchange, Dempsey landed a left, then a right to the face and Gene countered with a similar attack. As Jack came rushing in, Gene caught Dempsey's bad eye with a power wallop and the blood flowed more freely. The eye started to swell badly.

Round Eight. Dempsey began crowding Gene. Tunney retaliated by stabbing two beauties to Jack's face that caused him to halt in his tracks. Dempsey crouched low, looking for an opening, but Tunney caused him to back away as he struck home with a power right that struck the side of the head.

Gene's cleverness was now proving too much for his adversary. As Dempsey rushed forth and tossed a swing that missed, Gene caught him with a hard right to the body that slowed the titleholder.

Jack lunged in again, but Gene's cleverness caused him to miss. The rain had dropped to a light shower by now. That was welcomed by all. As Gene jabbed Jack's head with a left, the bell sounded.

Round Nine. Dempsey was refreshed after good work on the part of his seconds. He came forth for this round with much vigor. But Tunney, by now, was a very determined fighter. He knew he had the upper hand and wasn't going to lose it.

He countered every move of Dempsey. As Dempsey rushed in, tossing a right that missed, Tunney came up with a beautiful right uppercut to the jaw that checked Jack's rush.

The rain began to fall heavily again. Tunney kept jabbing and most of his efforts were accurate. Dempsey tossed a right, then a left, for Tunney's body but each missed.

As Jack came forth again, Gene caught him with a good right uppercut to the jaw that jarred the champion. Jack missed a wild right, then shot a left to Gene's stomach before they clinched.

Tunney forced Dempsey into his own corner where he connected with two heavy rights to Jack's jaw. A left to the body forced the champion to clinch again. Just before the bell clanged, two heavy rights to the jaw jarred the defending titleholder.

Round Ten. The last session opened with the rain falling heavily. The huge gathering roared for Tunney to finish the job. It was evident that only a knockout could save the crown for Dempsey.

Tunney landed a right to Jack's head. Dempsey rushed forth furiously but Tunney met his rush with a power right to the head, then Gene sent a blow to Jack's sore eye that closed it. Gene then landed several rights and lefts to the face and head. He knew he had the fight clinched but there was no letup as the finish neared.

Several uppercuts dazed Dempsey. Tunney was swinging to Dempsey's jaw as the bell sounded, ending the fight.

It was a unanimous decision, as both judges, Frank Brown and Mike Bernstein, ruled in Gene's favor.

The cheers that followed were as much for the fallen idol as for the newly crowned king. Tears dropped from Dempsey's eyes like the raindrops that fell throughout the battle.

Estelle was in the living room of their suite at the Adelphi Hotel when the beaten champion arrived with his handlers. She, of course, had heard the bad news. She looked at her husband's badly bruised face, then gently asked, "What happened, Ginsberg?"

"I just forgot to duck, honey," answered the ex-champ.

Tunney, a product of World War I, was now, at 29, the ruler of the heavyweight division. Gene, a man of ideals—"The Dreamer," many of the sportswriters had tagged him—now owned pugilism's highest honor. Following his victory, the ex-marine told the press:

"I had made up my mind I'd win. I aimed to prove to the skeptics that I was worthy of the match. I was tired of the criticism aimed at me by the press. I knew my capability and went into the ring determined to prove that I was a worthy contender."

It took a lot of courage for Tunney to accept that fight. But he had confidence in himself. He was certain, he told his friends, that he would win the crown. He had spent hours in his Stroudsburg, Pennsylvania, hideout studying Dempsey's ring battles from films he had obtained. He examined closely the fights with Brennan, Miske, Carpentier, and Firpo.

"In his fight with Firpo, Jack revealed himself an open target for a vicious punch," explained Tunney. "But he displayed tremendous hitting power, speed, and endurance. I made a close study of all these points and decided that Dempsey was not an invincible target as most reporters had written. My scrutiny of Jack's good and weak points is what enabled me to win the title."

In his book *Arms for Living,* Tunney has this to say of Dempsey:

"I played a small part in the postwar extravaganza, the Dempsey-Carpentier fight card, on which I fought in the semifinal with Soldier Jones, Canadian heavyweight champion. After the bout I watched the Dempsey-Carpentier affair. I had never seen Dempsey in the ring before. I noted the superb fighting physique of the champion. Those Dempsey shoulders, wide as a barn door, and pipe-stem legs attracted my attention.

"I saw the vicious attack, shifty stalking, the elusive bobbing, the swift sliding in, the short, heavy punches, the damaging body blows—they impressed me! To me it was obvious that Carpentier, light and inferior in punching power, was going to be defeated when Dempsey caught up with him.

"In that bout I learned a lot. I decided I could hit Dempsey with short righthand punches that would hurt him. That was confirmed when Jack fought Firpo. That I figured was Dempsey's weakness."

It will be recalled that expert opinion gave Tunney little chance to win the title. Odds were 11 to 5 against him, but Gene upset the applecart.

Unlike many other boxers, especially champions who have lost their titles, Dempsey had no excuses to offer after losing to Tunney. Gene had won the crown fairly. When I visited Manassa Jack in his hotel room, Dempsey said to me, "I don't want any sympathy. I don't need any. The better man won. I have no alibis to offer."

"Did the rain bother you?"

"No, nothing bothered me except what Tunney was doing to me. I had four stitches sewed over my left eye last night," he said. "It was an old cut reopened."

An article appeared in a Philadelphia paper in which the writer hinted that collusion was the cause of Jack's downfall. I asked Jack if he would answer the writer.

"I wouldn't dignify the report by denying it. I lost fairly. Let's not cook up phony excuses," he retorted.

Then Dempsey related that Rickard had spoken to him and asked whether he would be willing to fight Gene in a return engagement.

"I told Tex I was not ready to make a decision. I wanted some time. I was thinking of retiring, but when I told Rickard, he pleaded, 'Don't do it yet. There's a fortune in your return with Tunney. Give me a chance to put on another match with you and Gene.' "

Dempsey said he was not prepared at that time to accept Rickard's offer, but he would consider it.

That was all Rickard needed to set into motion the preliminaries for a Dempsey–Jack Sharkey bout, which eventually led to the return contest with Tunney.

Strange as it may seem, Tunney was the first heavyweight champion to enter the ring in a title defense in which the challenger on the day of the fight was the favorite. On the day before the return battle in Chicago, Gene was on even betting terms with ex-champ Jack. But on the day of the fight, the wagering shifted in Dempsey's favor, something unknown up until then in a heavyweight title match. From 2 to 1 in Gene's favor, to even money, to 6 to 5 in Dempsey's favor the odds had traveled. At fight time, wagering was back to even money.

In all of Dempsey's title defenses, the odds had favored him. As much as 7 to 1 was offered on him when he faced Miske. He was 4 to 1 to beat Brennan. Against Carpentier and Firpo, Manassa Jack was a 3 to 1 choice.

When the second Tunney fight was announced, Gene was favored 2 to 1, but it didn't take long for the odds to shift. They dropped with a sudden flood of Dempsey money, indicating that the public did not accept the Philadelphia fight as a true test. Something went wrong, they figured, which would be righted in the Chicago engagement. The public's judgment was almost proven correct.

24

FOLLOWING THE LOSS of his title to Tunney, Dempsey was prepared to call a halt to further fistic engagements. Urged by Estelle, he was tempted to become a slippers-and-pipe man. But Rickard had other plans. Jack had proven himself an excellent meal ticket for Tex, and Tex figured that Dempsey, despite his loss to Tunney, was still the best attraction in boxing. The promoter therefore decided to prep Jack for a return contest with Tunney by pitting him against an outstanding boxer in an elimination contest. The man he chose for that test was a promising 24-year-old named Jack Sharkey.

Dempsey's popularity had grown despite his defeat. Where the public had jeered him on previous occasions, now Jack had become an idol. In defeat he had gained the admiration and support of the fighting public. He'd even won over many of those who had previously booed him because of the draft charge during World War I.

Although this popularity proved an enigma to newsmen—or to many of them, at least—Rickard was not for one moment stymied by it. He was fully aware of the reasons behind this new acclaim and, accordingly, was hot on Dempsey's trail for a speedy comeback.

It took considerable urging on the promoter's part, but he finally convinced Dempsey that the public favored another contest with Tunney and would give it wholehearted support. But, added Tex, an elimination contest was necessary to arouse a deep interest in the return match. If, however, Sharkey should win, Rickard would have the man who beat Dempsey as an attraction against Tunney. Either way, the canny Rickard couldn't lose, though Dempsey, Tex figured, would be the better drawing card.

Sharkey, through his manager, Johnny Buckley, was giving Rickard a lot of trouble because he had been shunted to the sidelines. But now Tex was ready to take full advantage of all the circumstances by pitting Sharkey against Dempsey, the winner being rewarded with a match with Tunney. Buckley, however, was insistent that Sharkey was entitled to a title contest without an elimination. But Rickard convinced the manager that a buildup through such a bout would be the proper procedure since it would pave the way for two huge gate attractions instead of one. A powerful argument, indeed! That, plus Rickard's promise that Sharkey would get the next championship shot if he defeated Dempsey, enabled Tex to close the deal.

The buildup for another million-dollar gate was launched. It didn't take long for Rickard to be convinced that he did in fact have another million-dollar extravaganza on his hands, so quick was the response of the public once the buildup began and the tickets went on sale.

The bout was slated for the Yankee Stadium, July 21, 1927, the year that Babe Ruth ensured the Stadium's immortality with his 60 homers.

During the training period, Leo P. Flynn, now advising Dempsey, kept telling the press and Dempsey that Sharkey was overrated, overconfident, and showed weaknesses that would tell in favor of Dempsey.

Sharkey was overconfident, and that would spell disaster for him. The Lithuanian was a good hitter and fast boxer. He was powerful and owned a good record, including a victory, via a foul, in 13 rounds over Dempsey's nemesis, Harry Wills.

In addition, the Boston Gob had defeated a number of top heavyweights, such good fighting names as Eddie Huffman, King Solomon, George Godfrey, Mike McTigue, Homer Smith, Johnny Risko, and Jim Maloney.

By fight time, it was obvious that, once again, Rickard had displayed much foresight. The crowds pouring into the Stadium indicated that Tex's adventurous spirit had paid off extremely well.

Sharkey was stopped by Dempsey in the seventh round. A body blow which Sharkey and his followers insisted was a foul punch ended the fray and put Manassa Jack back into line as the leading contender.

Sharkey's strategy was to box at long range. Fast, strong, and an accurate jabber, he outboxed Dempsey, who, carrying 194½ pounds, displayed a lack of speed and kept losing ground as the bout progressed. The 196-pound Bay Stater was a tough nut for Dempsey to crack at this stage of his career. But he eventually did it, to the joy of his admirers and particularly to that of Rickard, who added to his promotions the fourth million-dollar gate.

At the time of the knockout, Dempsey was behind in points. His legs were growing wearier by the moment; his form was far from that of his heyday; the outlook grew dimmer for him with each round. Then came the punch that saved the day for the former heavyweight king. And then came a great hue and cry from Sharkey and many of his supporters. Several reporters also joined the concert.

Had Sharkey actually been knocked out or did Dempsey win on a foul punch? That was the question. For many days it was argued pro and con both in the press and wherever fight fans gathered.

The answer is that Dempsey won the fight legitimately. When the Boston Gob dropped his hands to his side in the fatal seventh and complained to the referee about Jack's blows, Dempsey quickly took advantage of the situation by hooking a powerful left to the jaw, the blow that terminated the contest.

Shouts of foul were immediately raised in Sharkey's corner, but Referee Jack O'Sullivan declared the punch was legal and counted Sharkey out.

Sharkey had done his best work in the second round. It was also one in which Dempsey's weaknesses were easy to behold.

Dempsey had sent over two stunning left hooks, but they didn't shake the Bostonian a bit. He backed away, rapidly came forward again, then ripped several hefty blows into Manassa Jack's body, making Dempsey wince. Sharkey also had much the better of an exchange that followed.

In the third round, in a brave attempt to even the score, Dempsey sailed into the loquacious Bay Stater and pumped away with punches that jarred him. Sharkey recoiled, but was apparently unhurt.

The most exciting session was the fifth, and Dempsey was the victim. In that frame, Sharkey laced crunching blows to Dempsey's stomach. Manassa Jack was able to cut Sharkey's eye, though.

In the sixth, Dempsey poked lefts and rights to the Boston sailor's body. But each time Sharkey was hit, he came forward with an attack of his own.

Then came the unforgettable seventh, which brought Dempsey back into the championship picture.

Again Dempsey's presence in a boxing match had brought in a gate of more than a million dollars. Receipts totaled $1,083,530. And watching the affair in the House that Ruth Built were 75,000 fans.

It didn't take long for Rickard to start arrangements for the Tunney-Dempsey return bout. This time, though, Manassa Jack would be the challenger, in a contest that would bring into boxing history both a new top in receipts and an international topic that has continued over the years—the "long count" controversy.

25

WITH DEMPSEY'S TRIUMPH came quick action by Rickard to consummate negotiations for a return engagement with Tunney. He had begun preliminary work on the encounter several months prior to Dempsey's bout with Sharkey.

Few in the boxing world, even among Gene's closest friends, knew that Tunney was thinking of retiring. New York State Athletic Commissioner William Muldoon and Rickard were confidants in Tunney's plans, and, at Gene's request, arrangements for the bout with Dempsey were quickly gotten under way.

Rickard received several tempting offers to stage the return in New York, Massachusetts, and Pennsylvania. But, months before the articles were signed, he had agreed with Illinois' politicians to stage the affair at huge Soldiers' Field, Chicago, on September 22, 1927, and to limit the bout to ten rounds.

A gathering of 104,943 paid the record sum of $2,658,660 to view the return engagement. Sportswriters, seeking a catch title for the contest, dubbed it "The Second Battle of the Century." It became the "Battle of the Long Count" following the controversial incident while Tunney was on the floor.

It was a contest of thrills furnished by each of the contestants. Gene was on the verge of a knockout in the historic seventh. In that round, after Dempsey had floored Tunney, the referee's action of not starting the count until Dempsey had reached a neutral corner added four seconds to the knockdown. Many of Dempsey's supporters were—and are to this day—of the opinion that the "long count" saved Tunney from a knockout. Gene, however, has always maintained he could have gotten to his feet before the fatal ten seconds would have been reached. Tunney has asserted, and correctly so, that since Referee Dave Barry was not counting, he had a perfect right to remain down while the count progressed. That was his prerogative and he took advantage of the delay.

After his victory, Tunney was to box once more before retiring. That final fight came against Tom Heeney on July 26, 1928, at New York's Yankee Stadium. Gene's last round as a fighter was the 11th, for in that round the ex-marine stopped Heeney, thereby retaining his heavyweight crown.

In the Tunney-Dempsey contest, Jack weighed 192½, Gene 189½. The majority of the writers gave Gene seven of the ten rounds. Legs weary and arms heavy, Dempsey was unable to connect with many of his best punches. Only sporadically did the former heavyweight king show flashes of the form that gave him the "killer" reputation.

Midway through the historic seventh round, Gene struck Jack with a right to the forehead, which aroused the true fighting spirit of the Manassa Mauler. Jack rushed forth, planting a right to Gene's jaw, a shot which forced the defending titleholder to the ropes where Dempsey then connected with a tremendous left that dropped Tunney to the canvas.

Now the old Dempsey, rarin' to go after his prey, stood over Gene and refused to obey the command of the referee to go to a neutral corner. It was only after a stubborn Jack obeyed that Referee Barry started counting, beginning at one, though Tunney had been down at least four seconds.

The delayed count may or may not have helped Gene to hold on to his crown, but many reporters, eyeing him keenly, were of the opinion that the extra time did save Tunney from a kayo.

Tunney and his supporters thought otherwise. I was sitting in the corner where Gene had been felled. Like several other reporters in the front row, among them Bill McGeehan of the *New York Tribune,* Hype Igoe of the *New York Journal,* Bill Farnsworth of the same paper, and Wurra Wurra McLaughlin of the *World,* all famous critics, I thought Barry's action had saved Tunney from losing the title.

Upon rising, Gene pranced around the ring, apparently none the worse for his experience. That riled Dempsey. Angered, he motioned to Gene to fight.

The delayed count gave Tunney the time he required to face Jack with a clear brain. And judging by his actions during the remainder of the round, Gene obviously had recovered sufficiently. He quickly fell into a clinch after Dempsey missed two rights. Seconds later, the bell clanged to end one of the most famous rounds in ring history.

The remainder of the bout was all in Gene's favor. He had battered Dempsey's face into a mess, but even so, Jack, except for weariness, did not suffer as badly as he did in the Philadelphia affair with Tunney. Besides which, Jack's marksmanship was more in evidence in this contest.

In the matter of ring science, however, Tunney had a big advantage. He was supreme. And too, he even floored Dempsey in the eighth round.

The round-by-round story of the "long count" battle follows:

Round One. Dempsey came out of his corner with a rush and crashed two lefts against Gene's jaw. Tunney retaliated with a right to the chin that tossed Jack's head back. Tunney followed with two hefty wallops, one to the jaw and the other to Jack's body that caused Dempsey to wince. Tunney followed his advantage by boring in and knocking Jack against the ropes with a left hook and a right to the head. Dempsey quickly turned and crashed a right to Gene's head, then a left to the face as the gong sounded. Dempsey asked for the smelling salts as he got to his corner.

Round Two. As the bell clanged, Dempsey rushed out of his corner and sent a savage blow to Gene's mouth that turned on the claret. It was a stunning left hook. The men exchanged blows furiously. Dempsey's attack forced Gene to the ropes. Jack acted like one in a frenzy.

A right to Gene's body again forced him against the ropes. Dempsey then rushed Gene into a neutral corner where he landed a power left to the shoulder. Tunney rocked Jack with two rights to the jaw and Dempsey landed on the ropes.

Jack continued to force the fighting, but Gene was keeping him back with a flock of snappy lefts to the head and body. Dempsey was leaning back on the ropes as the bell sounded.

Round Three. Dempsey was slow in coming out of his corner. He missed a right to the head and Tunney jabbed him several times. Tunney's right and left to the body slowed up Jack. Dempsey came weaving in, but Gene staggered him with a right uppercut and a right straight to the face. Dempsey now was bleeding from nose and mouth.

Round Four. Dempsey came running out of his corner and almost knocked Gene over the top strand with a wild left swing. Jack then swarmed all over Gene and nearly floored him. A right and left to the head and a left to the stomach caused Tunney to back into his corner. Dempsey swung a right and nearly went down when he missed.

Gene opened a cut over Dempsey's right eye with a beautiful left as Dempsey was coming in for a clinch. For the first time, Gene forced Jack to step back and box.

Jack ripped a short right uppercut to Gene's jaw that jarred the champion, then followed with a right to the ear which drew the claret. Dempsey now started to hit Gene on the back of the neck. Jack was warned by the referee. Gene staggered Jack with a bombardment of lefts and rights and the challenger was bleeding badly as the gong sounded.

Round Five. Dempsey weaved out of his corner and danced around Tunney. Gene missed a left and went into a clinch. As Dempsey was short with a left to the body, Gene backed away.

Gene blocked a power left for the body and countered with an uppercut that raised a lump on Jack's head.

Now, for the first time, Tunney was forcing the fight. He staggered the challenger with a left to the jaw, then showered him with lefts and rights to the head and body that had Dempsey in a bad way.

A right to the jaw jarred Dempsey. Gene followed with two rights to the body as the round ended.

Round Six. Dempsey came out and clouted Gene to a neutral

corner. Gene was knocked against the ropes by a flurry of lefts and rights to the body. Dempsey was now grunting with every punch, indicating his eagerness to put his man away, but finding Gene tough. Gene complained to the referee about Dempsey's roughness in the clinches and the official warned Jack. Dempsey was tired. That gave Gene another opportunity to open a good body attack.

The champion was now breathing heavily. Dempsey stepped in and rocked his opponent with rights and lefts to the head and body, very effective blows. They came forth like rifle shots, but didn't land with sufficient force to put Gene down.

Round Seven. Dempsey came out of his corner with determination, but Gene checked his advance and Manassa Jack held. He put Gene back on his heels at the break with a power right to the jaw. Gene landed against the ropes, then, after absorbing a tremendous left to the jaw, went down with a look of dismay. He was bleary-eyed as he fell. He appeared dazed as Referee Barry ordered Dempsey to a neutral corner, a command he failed to obey until the count of four had been reached by the official timer. When Jack finally heeded Barry's command, the count was begun again, but at one. Four seconds had been wasted by Dempsey's slow action.

Gene had by then moved to a rest position and was listening to the referee's toll. He got to his feet by nine. He began retreating around the ring with Dempsey, angry, following him.

"Come on and fight," called a scowling Manassa Jack to Gene.

Dempsey missed a right swing and went back on his heels from a left to the body. A momentary exchange brought cheers from the spectators. It appeared now that Dempsey was tiring, although his fighting heart was still functioning. A left hook sent Dempsey against the ropes. Jack missed a number of punches as Tunney kept circling the ring. Tunney landed a left hook to Jack's head as the bell sounded.

Round Eight. Tunney came out and started boxing on the retreat. Dempsey went after him. Dempsey missed a wild left swing. Tunney jabbed lightly then retreated.

As they broke from a clinch, Dempsey's right eye was cut. Angered, Manassa Jack went after Gene but couldn't get a clean shot at him. Dempsey kept bobbing and weaving and Tunney kept standing him off.

Dempsey found that Gene had fully recovered from the knockdown in the seventh and was getting the upper hand. Tunney floored Jack with a right chop to the head for a count of one. Gene was calm and maneuvering in a manner that made Jack miss frequently. Jack tried to corner Gene, but failed.

Round Nine. Jack came dashing out of his corner. As Dempsey came forward, Gene drove a right to Jack's head, then fell into a clinch. On the break. Tunny snapped three stiff jabs to Jack's face and the blood flowed. Dempsey's left eye started to bleed. Gene went after it and popped away with stiff jabs. He then hit Jack twice with power punches that sent the Manassa Mauler against the ropes. Tunney jabbed with his left, then landed twice with rights to the face.

Those were followed with two stiff rights to the jaw that had Dempsey staggering. Dempsey's nose was a red smear as he came to his corner. The round was a good one for Tunney.

Round Ten. They shook hands. Dempsey missed a left hook, then pushed Gene. Jack was missing badly. He was overeager and Gene took advantage of the situation. Playing safe, knowing that he had the fight, Gene pounded Jack's face several times with lefts and rights and stood off Dempsey's rushes with good jabbing. Jack's face was now a bloody mess. He bobbed and weaved, his customary style, but Gene's jabs prevented Manassa Jack from connecting. Dempsey was staggered several times. The bell sounded with Jack looking as he never did before.

He put on his robe and congratulated Gene as Referee Barry held up the champion's hand in token of victory.

Again Rickard's fabulous promotion had gone far beyond expectations. The number of spectators was not as large as that attending the Philadelphia enterprise, but the receipts far exceeded those of the Quaker City venture. The enormous total of $2,658,660 was a new high. It was the fifth time in Rickard's promotions that more than a million dollars had been paid to see a world heavyweight boxing match, and the first that reached two million.

Borne on the wings of radio, the report of that fight was heard in half the world over 79 broadcasting stations. The report was arranged by the *New York Evening Telegram.* The broadcast was heard in England. Legionnaires received the report in France. In Australia, boxing fans gave up their lunch period to hear Graham McNamee's description. When dawn arose over the African veldt, people learned that Tunney had retained his crown. South Americans paused over their coffee to hear news from Soldiers' Field. In Germany, the voice of McNamee was picked up and rebroadcast through Stuttgart so that the owners of the humblest crystal set might follow the tide of battle. It was the first such hookup for any sports event.

But beyond these *firsts,* the Chicago contest, sadly, officially marked the end of Dempsey's pugilistic career. Though but 32, he knew the time had come to hang up the gloves. There would be exhibitions, many in fact, but, well . . . that's not the same thing.

The historic "long count" remains an epic in the history of the heavyweight division. No controversy in the annals of boxing has caused such widespread discussion over the years.

Was Tunney's title saved by the action of Referee Barry?

Did Dempsey fail to regain the title due to a technicality?

If so, it was due to Jack's own negligence. In such a case, that his failure to go to a neutral corner proved extremely costly is a gross understatement.

It had been agreed that should a knockdown take place, the one scoring it would immediately go to a neutral corner. This Dempsey did not do. He was too anxious and that perhaps cost him the opportunity to regain the throne. I was present when the rule was discussed with representatives of both Gene and Jack in the offices of the Illinois State Athletic Commission.

That body, following the protest by Dempsey's representatives, declared that the knockdown rule had been put into the regulations for that bout for the first time at the urgent request of Dempsey's representatives. It read:

"When a knockdown occurs, the timekeeper shall immediately rise and announce the seconds audibly as they elapse. The referee shall first see that the opponent retires to the farthest corner and then, turning to the timekeeper, shall pick up the count in unison with the timekeeper, announcing the seconds to the boxer reclining on the ring floor. Should the boxer who scored the knockdown fail to remain in the neutral corner, the referee and timekeeper shall cease counting until he has so retired."

The rule, as then enforced, differed from that of New York, where it had originated. In New York, the referee picks up the count of the official knockdown timer as soon as the boxer who has scored the knockdown has retired to the neutral corner. In the Empire State, the referee does not begin the count over again as did Barry.

Since both Tunney and Dempsey, through their chief seconds, had agreed to the Illinois rule the day prior to the fight, Tunney was well within his rights to remain down and Referee Barry should not have been accused of giving Dempsey "the works."

Ironically, although Jack, through his own fault, failed to follow the rule, thus perhaps throwing away a chance for a knockout, he nevertheless became the Man of the Hour.

Bob Edgren, sitting next to me, held his stopwatch on the knockdown and counted 18 seconds before Gene got off the floor. My stopwatch registered 14 seconds. That of Hype Igoe of the *New York Journal*, who also was sitting next to me, ticked off 18 seconds. Thus the timing for the knockdown differed.

The "long count" episode brought about the establishment of a new rule, one that makes it mandatory for the referee to pick up the count from the official knockdown timer only after the contestant who had scored it goes to a neutral corner.

Although Jack Kearns no longer had a financial interest in Dempsey, he was quite upset at what took place during the "long count."

"The judges and referee had nothing to do with the result," said Kearns. "His handlers should have shooed him away. Were I on the job, I would have had Jack out of the ring on his way to the dressing room, instead of waiting for Referee Barry to shoo Jack to his corner. At any rate, Referee Barry definitely should have given Jack the benefit of the four seconds already counted instead of starting the count over again.

"Had I been in Dempsey's corner that night, I'd have landed into the ring as I did in Toledo and I'd have taken Jack out and this time I would not have gotten him to return to resume the fight."

Dempsey has always refused to belittle Tunney's victory, declaring the verdict a fair one.

"I was told of the rule and should have obeyed it," Jack told me. "I suppose a jungle fighter cannot change."

Dempsey told me that Tunney had offered him a third bout but that he declined it. Jack explained that at the time he had scar tissue that had reached the danger point. Jack was therefore not eager to take any chances.

"Your eyesight will be impaired to a dangerous point," his eye specialist had warned him. He urged, convincingly, Jack to give up further ring activity. Dempsey obeyed. He's always been of the opinion that his decision to retire was a good one.

"Had I desired to continue boxing," Jack informed me, "Rickard would have been the promoter. He told me so. He said a third bout would have drawn the biggest crowd in ring history. However, I wasn't interested in fighting Gene again.

"With me out, Gene, as you know, took on Tom Heeney in the final contest of his career."

I was in Rickard's office when the topic of a third bout with Tunney was discussed.

"It's a match I'd like to make," said Rickard. "It will outdraw any sports event ever held. It will draw a million dollars more than any sports event ever staged. It's a natural after what has happened."

"Do you think Gene will go through with it if Jack consents?" I asked.

"It isn't Gene I'm worried about. He's willing. It's Jack. I can't induce him to change his mind. He says he wants to retire and now I'm sure that's what he's going to do. Until this morning I was certain I could get Dempsey to change his mind. But I learned a short time ago that there isn't a chance. That's why I have decided on a Tunney-Heeney bout. Gene had promised Tom a crack at the title if Tunney beat Dempsey again, and now he has it."

Tunney's acceptance of Heeney as an opponent followed the announcement of Dempsey that he had hung up his gloves and henceforth would appear only in exhibitions and as a referee.

Jack's retirement brought high praise from Tunney in various interviews.

Jack and Gene have remained very friendly over the years. When Gene's son, John—now a United States senator—entered a congressional race in California, Dempsey went out to campaign for him. The Tunney habit prevailed, as John won.

26

THE DEFEAT of Dempsey in the return engagement with Tunney spelled the end of Jack's career as a fighting man, but not the end of Jack's importance to the boxing world.

After the death of Tex Rickard on January 6, 1929, the Garden promoters asked Dempsey to act as promoter of the Jack Sharkey–Young Stribling fight, slated for the following month, February 27, in Miami, which Rickard had started. Dempsey agreed to act as front man, with Steve Hannagan, a top publicist, Sid Mercer of the *New York Journal,* and me aiding him.

The fight drew a record gathering of 483 newsmen from all parts of the world. They had made the journey to see whether the death of Rickard had placed the Garden outfit in a precarious position. Each was eager to observe firsthand whether the directors could carry on the work of the leading sports promotion organization in the world now that its leader had passed away.

The Sharkey-Stribling affair was a promotional success. Later, however, similar ventures in Chicago and New York fell flat. Not until the Schmeling-Baer fight in 1933 did Dempsey make good on his own as a promoter.

If in the early years of his retirement Dempsey wasn't exactly a record-setter in the promotional field, he did find success in the ring—as a referee. In fact, his popularity as a referee enabled him to gross $322,000 over a period of half a year in 1931. And it all began in—Iowa, Davenport, Iowa, in the office of promoter and friend C. W. (Red) Henaghan.

Henaghan approached Dempsey and his business manager, Leonard Sacks, with a proposition for Dempsey to referee a fight.

"I'm in a tight spot, Jack," said Henaghan, "and I need your help. My fight isn't going too good. Come to my arena and referee the main event. You can put the promotion over for me. I'll pay you $2,000 and give you two round-trip tickets. Please, Jack, do it for me."

After considerable persuasion, the deal was made. Jack and Leonard were about to leave when the latter remarked to Henaghan:

"Dempsey will be on hand. He'll referee. If you have a good house, give Jack 50 percent; if the show is a flop, give us nothing."

They shook hands on the deal, and Dempsey and Sacks were on their way, laughing.

On the night of the fight the arena was jammed. The gate reached $10,800, an unheard-of figure for that arena, which had never grossed more than $7,000. The promoter thanked Jack and handed him 50 percent of the gate as he had promised. Jack turned it down. He told the promoter the original fee of $2,000 was sufficient.

"Let's stick to that," said Sacks.

As Sacks explained to me later: "I didn't realize until then what a tremendous card Dempsey was, even after he had lost the championship. That promoter taught Jack and me something. I now realized how much the champ meant to a promoter even though he no longer had that title. It was that incident which eventually enabled us to clean up a third of a million in six months. Beat that if you can in fight promotion!"

Henceforth, Dempsey was seen as a referee throughout the country, working such cities as Wichita, Kansas City, Oklahoma City, Toledo, Birmingham, Atlanta, Fort Wayne, and Tulsa. In all, he acted as a referee in 87 cities. Jack's fee was usually $2,500. In every instance the promoter was well repaid with excellent turnouts.

During this successful half-year period of refereeing, the roar of the crowd, the smell of the ring, his own popularity with the fans—all these things began to gnaw away at Jack. That yearning once again to don the gloves was getting to him. Could he do it? Did he dare gamble on a comeback at his age, 36?

There was but one way to find out whether he still possessed the stamina, speed, and other qualifications a fighter should have when taking on the best in his division. So, with Sacks as his mentor, Jack hit the exhibition trail in earnest. If he had it, fine. If not, well, the money would ease the pain. From his recent refereeing experience he was certain the crowds would come out to watch him.

He guessed right. Wherever the ex-champ appeared, sellout gatherings were the rule. Watching Dempsey on the exhibition trail, one was reminded of John L. Sullivan when the Bay Stater toured the country so successfully.

On February 18, 1932, in Chicago, Jack came to the realization that he didn't have it. That night, in Chicago Stadium before 23,332, he faced King Levinsky in a four-round bout, which was billed as an exhibition. It was, however to serve as a trial run for Manassa Jack. Levinsky, a fairly tough boy, weighed in at 196½, Jack at 190. The fight went the limit, with Dempsey not looking very good. Ideas of a comeback were laid to rest.

The name of Dempsey could still set records, though. Official receipts for the bout came to $74,199, the largest gate for an indoor match up to that time. Jack's share was $33,000.

Dempsey had momentarily forgotten one of boxing's axioms: "They never come back."

Most of those who, after retirement, have attempted a comeback have failed.

Four years after his annihilation at the hands of Dempsey, Jess Willard made a comeback try. The Pottawatomie Giant stopped Floyd Johnson in the 11th round, but two months later was kayoed by Firpo in eight. His comeback aspirations were also kayoed.

In 1910, six years after his retirement, Jim Jeffries attempted to wrest from Jack Johnson's head the crown he once wore. Johnson knocked out the Boilermaker in 15. Exit Jeffries.

And now Dempsey's name was added to the list.

Despite his disappointment over the Levinsky outcome, Jack did continue fighting exhibitions. The money was good —great, in fact! Prior to facing Levinsky in February 1932, Dempsey had from August 1931 to January 1932 drawn 230,155 paid admissions, totaling a gross of $477,260. Jack's share was $246,066.

Some of the names Jack faced following the Levinsky battle were Pat Sullivan, Jack Phillips, George Trenkle, Ray Vanzke, Ed Williams, Fred Taylor, Tim Charles, Jack O'Dowd, Tiny Powell, and Frankie Wine. The majority would have made good sparmates for Manassa Jack in his heyday.

Dempsey enjoyed his exhibition tour, but all too often he found himself back in the glory days. But then, perhaps not all too often. Jack realized that those days had put him on top, that the glory days had given him success both then and now. Why should he forget a time in his life that changed him from an impoverished nobody to one whose name was respected wherever boxing was known? As he put it:

"The station I enjoy in life may be traced to about three hours of appearances in the ring. That I figure is the total of actual time spent in my major ring battles. Those include the knockouts of Jess Willard, Georges Carpentier, Luis Firpo, Jack Sharkey, and the two fights I had with Gene Tunney. Those contests eventually transformed me from a drifter to a person who is welcomed wherever he goes."

Jack and Estelle were divorced in 1931. Two years later Dempsey married singer Hannah Williams. By Hannah, Jack had two daughters, Barbara and Joan.

Dempsey and Hannah were divorced in 1943. Jack received custody of his two daughters when referee J. Addison Young awarded him an interlocutory decree. The jurist ruled that Dempsey's accusation that his wife had been unfaithful to him "was proven beyond a doubt."

27

"I'VE LICKED tougher guys than Jack Dempsey."

The speaker—Cowboy Luttrell. The year—1940.

Dempsey, Max Waxman—Jack's friend and business manager—and I were in Atlanta, Georgia, for a fight that Max had arranged in which the former champion was to face Cowboy Luttrell. The contest might best be described as a grudge exhibition. Luttrell, a wrestler, had challenged Dempsey to settle things with gloves after Jack had clashed with him while refereeing a wrestling match.

Luttrell was popular in the South, and the guarantee was an excellent one for Dempsey. He was to receive $10,000 and expenses for himself and Waxman. He asked me to act as referee and I agreed.

On the afternoon of the affair, after Jack and the Cowboy had weighed in publicly, I discussed the rules with both. I was not too eager to officiate, since Luttrell was a tough hombre, wild, one for whom rules meant nothing. He had his own rules and they were to rough it up and terminate the bout by any means possible.

I was quite emphatic in my instructions. I warned Luttrell, whose reputation for roughness was well known, that I would disqualify him should he resort to such.

Following my instructions, the sports editor of the *Atlanta Journal* asked Luttrell whether he was scared.

"Scared a who?" he inquired. "I've licked tougher guys than Jack Dempsey. I know many wrestlers who can lick him and I think I'm one of 'em. There never was a boxer who could beat a good wrestler."

In an edition of the *Atlanta Constitution,* Luttrell's boast received considerable attention. Dempsey saw the article and was angry.

"He made a big mistake giving out that story," said Jack. "He'll learn fast tonight who is boss."

On the evening of July 1, 1940, the arena was jammed. Jack, the Cowboy, and I entered the ring. Lusty cheers greeted the Manassa Mauler.

I gave the men their instructions. I warned Luttrell again not to make use of the usual rough stuff seen in wrestling matches.

The gong sounded and they were on their way.

Dempsey quickly got off his stool. He rushed forward. He let go a swinging left that caught Luttrell behind the ear.

The Cowboy was dazed. For almost a minute Luttrell, after regaining his equilibrium, walked around the ring, Dempsey following him.

"Stand up and fight," growled Jack, but Luttrell had had a taste of Jack's punches and had no desire to take any more such wallops. The bell came to his rescue. A disgusted look on Dempsey's face indicated to me that the end was in sight.

My guess was correct. At the clang of the gong for the second round, Jack rushed forward, planting a crushing blow on the Cowboy's chin. As Luttrell dropped his guard, a powerful right struck his jaw and he went flying through the ropes. His body was caught between the first and second strands and his feet were off the floor. As I hurried forward for the count, I tripped, and while on one knee, I counted Luttrell out.

The huge gathering cheered lustily—although the bout was over in a little more than four minutes. The spectators were satisfied. They had seen the Manassa Mauler in action. It was with difficulty that the champ made his way to the dressing room. In a few hours we were on our way to Chattanooga.

Tales of Dempsey's travels and exploits and popularity could fill a volume. An experience in Canada well illustrates his popularity, a popularity that has not diminished with the years.

World War II had ended. Dempsey was on his own again. Under the management of Max Waxman, the former world heavyweight champ made many appearances at businessmen's functions, hospitals, and charity affairs in many parts of the country. His popularity, like that of Joe Louis, had grown and the demands on his time likewise had increased.

Jack, accompanied by his business manager and me, was in Montreal in the late 1940s, where he was to referee the main event of a charity show. I was to officiate in the semifinal. Upon our arrival at the hotel, we found our passage to the entrance blocked by a cheering gathering. It was only after some effort that we gained entrance to the hotel lobby.

Once inside, Jack was mobbed with autograph seekers. A path was finally cleared and the management got our party into the reception room where local celebrities, including the mayor of Montreal, had gathered to greet the champion.

Since Dempsey had another engagement as a referee in Baltimore two days later, we agreed to make our exit from Canada as early after the fight as possible, for the return to New York. Our work as ring officials ended, we quickly returned to our hotel and prepared for the trip home.

It was now close to two o'clock in the morning and the long journey to New York was not too appealing. When we reached the customs depot, we failed to declare two gifts. We had made no purchases. However, we did have a beautiful deerskin which had been presented to Dempsey by a member of the Montreal Chamber of Commerce. Dempsey had been told by the mayor of Montreal that no declaration was necessary.

"Tell the inspector that it is a gift," he said.

We also received a case of liquor from the chamber of commerce. The stop at the exit station was made. Two inspectors approached and asked if we had anything to declare.

"Did you purchase anything?" one queried.

Our answer was in the negative. One of the inspectors was inquisitive. He was suspicious.

"You all are sure you have nothing to declare?" he again asked.

"Nothing," Max Waxman answered, angrily. "We have only a deerskin which the mayor gave to Mr. Dempsey as a gift and one case of Scotch given to us by your chamber of commerce."

"Well, let's open the bags for inspection," the inspector continued.

Our car was loaded with clothes. After a quick examination of the bags and car trunk, the inspectors scrutinized the deerskin.

"A fine skin," one remarked. "It must have cost you a lot of money."

"Inspector," Dempsey cut in, "we told you we bought nothing in Canada. This skin was a gift to me from your mayor."

"I'm afraid you are in trouble," continued the inspector.

Waxman turned on the inspector and in anger remarked:

"This is Mr. Jack Dempsey, the ex-heavyweight boxing champion. He came here to act as an official for your charity fights. If you don't believe us, it's easy to find out if our statement is correct."

"So you are Jack Dempsey," said the inspector with a sneer. "I'm the prime minister of Canada."

Before Waxman could go any further, I flashed my New York reporter's police card for identification. The inspector examined it, returned it, and, smiling, said to Dempsey, "Why didn't you tell me you are Jack Dempsey? Who won the fight?" he asked.

Then he replaced the contents of our bags except the deerskin, which Dempsey put in the trunk. Jack and I received a handshake from the inspectors. As Waxman was about to close the trunk, the inspector who was causing the difficulty turned to him and offered some advice:

"In the future, it will be much better if, when you come for an inspection, you declare everything you are taking back to your country."

As we were about to start for the border, Jack, turning to Waxman, remarked:

"Max, we've got the liquor in the trunk. That's enough to take home. Let's give the deerskin to the inspectors."

So it ended. Dempsey got out of the car, walked over to the chief inspector, handed him the deerskin with our compliments, and off we went on our return journey.

"That was an experience such as I have never before encountered in my many trips to Canada," Dempsey said, relieved.

I was in Chicago with Jack in September 1952 when he received a call from the warden of the Cook County jail asking Manassa Jack to entertain the inmates with some reminiscences.

The following day Jack and I went to the prison. The inmates were gathered in an auditorium where entertainment was on tap.

As Dempsey stepped forward to begin his talk, the warden remarked:

"There will be no cheers or handclapping until Mr. Dempsey completes his talk. Those are the rules."

About a minute after Jack's talk had been completed, bedlam broke loose. Many of the inmates attempted to get to the rostrum but were halted by the guards. A few got up front to shake the hand of "Mighty Jack." The warden, turning to Dempsey, said:

"They'll remember this for a long time, Jack. It was a pleasure to have you here. I hope you can come again to talk to them."

One prisoner asked Jack if he had won the second fight with Tunney in Chicago.

"Twenty-five years ago tomorrow, I received a tough break. At least it seemed so at the time," answered Dempsey. "But it turned out to be the greatest thing that could have happened to me. I refer to the 'long count.' I made the mistake of not walking to a neutral corner when I had Gene down and possibly out.

"Everybody blamed Referee Dave Barry and to this day many continue to do so, yet I was to blame, not Barry. I didn't obey the rules and I deserved the penalty. From that day I became a hero. Everybody greets me with friendly hands.

"Now this is the lesson I want to leave with you men. Make

the best of your situation. Keep your heads up. Things will straighten themselves out for you. Don't hold a grudge."

Then the warden and Jack went on a tour of the prison, which included a visit to Death Row. Warden John Babb told the newsmen accompanying Dempsey:

"We never had such excitement here. It is the best thing for discipline that has taken place here in years."

28

THE STIGMA caused by Jack's draft problem in World War I was finally erased in World War II. In 1942 the 47-year-old Dempsey enlisted in the Coast Guard, and served as a lieutenant commander in the Pacific theater. In accepting him, the Medical Corps officers marveled at his physical fitness.

Dempsey became an instructor in self-defense and jujitsu, and also did a great deal of refereeing. He was stationed for a time on ships that shuttled between various Pacific ports. Later he saw some service in the European zone.

One incident aboard the USS *Wakefield* stands out in Jack's memory. While refereeing a boxing match, a huge lumbering heavyweight scaling 220 pounds was making it tough for Jack. The sailor was an arrogant fellow, eager to stir up trouble and to exhibit his prowess.

"He was a good, tough scrapper," said Jack in recounting the story. "He swaggered around the boat, chest out, arms swinging, head held high, always a chip on his shoulders, always looking for a sucker foe. We had a good card arranged to entertain the boys and I was assigned to referee most of the bouts which the officer in charge had arranged.

"The sailor had appeared in several contests prior to that day, and being a socker, the tars gave him a good hand when it was announced that he would be seen in a contest that afternoon. Instead of one, he engaged in three bouts, each a three-rounder, and each against gobs smaller and lighter than he was. His opponents took a shellacking, but as a balm to the last one, who had received some heavy wallops, I called the bout a draw.

"That decision aroused the real winner. He leaped forth as if ready to tear me apart. He snarled as he pointed his finger at me and shouted:

" 'You know damn well I won the fight. What do you mean, a draw! I can lick anyone on this ship and that includes you!'

"With that he held up his fists, but I laughed at him. It was all part of the ship entertainment and I didn't think he would take my action seriously. When he continued to harass me, I scowled and told him to forget it. But he didn't.

"As an officer, I kept my temper. An officer is expected to forget personalities.

"The boys on the ship kept urging the fighter on. They were eager to see me take him on as he kept taunting me and daring me to engage him in a match. I finally did, just to save my reputation with the boys."

The deck was loaded with sailors, marines, and officers and all were anxious to see what Dempsey would do.

"I had to save my reputation with the guys," said the champ as he continued the story, "so I put on the gloves with him. We agreed to fight three rounds. He gave me a good shellacking in the opening round. He pasted me with some hefty swings.

"Then came the turning point. The sailor came moving in for what he figured would be the kill. I quickly sidestepped, changed my stance, let go a right to his body, then a left hook that doubled him up. He dropped like a log. The sailors yelled with delight. They thumped each other gloriously.

"I stood and laughed as I watched several members of the crew carry him to his corner. Then I looked down at my hands, which I had hurt. I was receiving a handsome ovation from the crew, so I held up my hand and, with a broad grin, said, 'See, I'm not yet finished.'

"At any rate, it was a good show. The tension on the ship was eased by the entertainment we had furnished. For the remainder of our voyage, that gob and I were pretty good friends. In fact, several times I gave him a few pointers on boxing. It was all good fun."

"On D Day in Okinawa, as our troops approached the mainland," said Dempsey, recalling another of his wartime experiences, "the craft members had their eyes peeled on the hills. They all had their weapons prepared in the event an emergency arose, but fortunately the ships came through without damage.

"We were in several boats about to land, when one lad, seeing me, shouted, 'Look, fellers, there's Jack Dempsey.' I was happy to be recognized and to be greeted by those boys. After we had landed and settled down, it was my pleasure to sign my name to a large number of items—envelopes, cigarette boxes, letters from home some were carrying, small autograph books, anything handy. They kept me pretty busy doing an enjoyable job. Many of those kids never saw our shores again."

When Dempsey was sent on a tour of the South Pacific combat area, he took with him, at my request, the film *Kings of the Ring,* which my friend Manny Baum and I had produced. The film, first of its kind ever screened, showed highlights of the world's most thrilling ring battles. It made a big hit with the servicemen.

The fight that created the greatest interest was that between Dempsey and Willard. There was Jack, hero of the battle, standing before his audience, giving the servicemen the highlights of the fight in which he had won the world heavyweight crown. The gobs and marines loved it.

With the red-hot fight film as a second in his corner, Jack scored a victory far greater than any he had won during his brilliant career between the ropes.

The tour in the South Pacific lasted four months, during which Jack visited thousands of servicemen in Australia, Okinawa, and a few other places. By tour's end, Dempsey was the one who had been cheered, for he gained the wholehearted support of Uncle Sam's fighting men.

A few days before Dempsey went on his trip to the South Pacific, I had a call from Washington telling me that three Secret Service agents were on their way to New York to visit me. They wished to discuss an espionage case in which, they informed me, at least one of the individuals was known to have visited my office. The agents had come to New York to inspect *The Ring*'s picture files, which contained thousands of photographs of boxers, many from Germany and France.

When the agents arrive, they requested absolute secrecy for their visit. They mentioned the names of two German pugilists who had been to our country, one of whom I had visited in Hamburg, Germany. They showed me a photo in which I was posing with the boxer. That was taken back in 1930, after I had severed my connections with the *New York Telegram.*

At the time of the German's arrival in the States, I had snapped several shots of him and his manager, who had accompanied him. I recalled that the manager had informed me he had a sister living in Kansas City, a woman I later had met in New York when she visited that city.

I was informed by the Secret Service agents that both the fighter and the manager had come to New York as agents for the German government and their apprehension was of great importance. We hunted through our files and after a search of about three hours, I located a photo of the manager. I informed the agents that I had introduced him to Tom McArdle, matchmaker of Madison Square Garden. A few days after McArdle had arranged for a six-round fight for the German fighter, both boxer and manager had disappeared and I had not seen them since.

However, a search of my files resulted in finding a letter from the manager's sister thanking me for courtesies extended. That I turned over to the agents. It had a Brooklyn postmark. With that as a lead, the inspectors and I visited the Coast Guard training camp where Dempsey was an officer and the search was on for the Germans. We were greeted by Dempsey who was not apprised of our mission. Two days later Jack left for his trip abroad while our search continued.

About two weeks after Jack's departure, I learned of the whereabouts of the manager's sister and two days later the agents located her. Through information gained, we found her brother and three other agents in a Long Island munitions plant, where all were placed under arrest on espionage charges. Two were later electrocuted in Sing Sing prison. Only recently the last of the quartet was released from prison, after having served a long term.

29

DEMPSEY WAS A GOOD LOSER in the ring, as Gene Tunney can testify. But once inside the ropes, he neither asked nor gave quarter. He was a battler of the old school, but when the fight was terminated, the scowl went with it, win or lose.

In Chicago, for example, when queried about the "long count" in the Tunney fight, he said, "The decision has been rendered. That's the end of it."

"Who staggered you most?" I inquired. "Was it Tunney?"

"That's an easy question. Willard tossed his big paw deep into my midsection in Toledo. Brother, I felt that punch! The effects remained with me for several days.

"But when it comes to a man-sized wallop, a stingeroo, the rap I received from Big Jess was only a tap compared with the dynamite that Gunboat Smith exploded on me in San Francisco. It caught me on the jaw and I saw stars all around me."

Discussing people he meets daily, friends and acquaintances and strangers who drop into his restaurant, Dempsey remarked:

"I find something good in all folks. We all have our faults, some worse than others, and we all have our good points, some better than most."

That philosophy is what Dempsey practices in his daily life when he is confronted by strangers who try to impose on his good nature. He got writer's cramp in his restaurant signing autographs, after which he decided on an easier way. He had his signature imprinted on a reproduction of the mural painted on the wall of his restaurant. The mural depicts a scene from his fight with Willard.

Max Waxman told about a stop in Provo, Utah, on the way to California, where Jack wanted to spend a few days with his daughters.

"We were tired and stopped in a town for refreshments and gas," Waxman reminisced.

"We weren't out of the car for more than a few minutes when we were surrounded by people requesting an autograph or a handshake. Fortunately, the chief of police was there and, realizing Jack's plight, requested the folks to let Jack and me cross the road to a hamburger stand.

"No sooner were we at the stand than again we were surrounded by a mob. Some wanted Jack to answer boxing queries; others, to obtain his signature. Still others merely wanted to be able to tell the folks back home they had seen the great Jack Dempsey. There was no way for us to get on our way again until Jack had taken care of his admirers.

"Jack told some yarns which hit the bull's-eye for many in that crowd. At times, I think the man is daffy the way he lets some people take advantage of him."

We were sitting in Dempsey's restaurant late one afternoon when three men approached Waxman and informed him they had come from Scranton, Pennsylvania, to request Jack's appearance as a referee in a charity show.

"What's in it for Jack?" asked Waxman.

"Nothing," replied one of the visitors, "other than his expenses."

"Well, friends," countered Waxman, "we'd like to oblige you but if we do it for you, we've got to do the same for others who come here with similar requests. He will have to be paid."

That reply appeared to be sufficient, but Waxman later learned otherwise.

"When I dropped in to see Jack in his apartment that evening," said Waxman, "there were the three guys from Scranton having dinner with Jack. Dempsey saw me shake my head in astonishment and said:

" 'Sit down and have dinner with us, Max. I think you know these gentlemen. You met them this afternoon. I just told them they can count on my going to Scranton to referee their fight. You know, it's a charity bout.'

" 'For nothing, Jack?' I asked.

" 'Yes, Max, it's a charity show. It's for a fine cause. Besides, I have a number of friends in Scranton and it will be nice to see them.'

"I laughed, then left the room, wondering to myself when he would learn not to give away his assets. He'll learn some day, I hope."

I told Jack what Max had said and he grinned. "Well, Nat, I find something good in the worst people, and something bad in the best. I like people."

This has been his attitude over the years. He has made it a practice to be quick to help a friend in need, though he's not always so quick to talk about it.

He did tell me, after some coaxing, about a visit he received from Bill Tate, his trainer in the Willard fight. Bill, a giant Negro, was working as a night watchman in Chicago. Dempsey, accompanied by his business manager, Leonard Sacks, arrived in the city to referee a fight. Jack was staying at the Morrison Hotel and Tate went there to greet him.

Bill was in ill health. He had been suffering from a chest ailment. He went to the hotel both to pay his respects to Jack and to seek aid.

"What would you like best?" asked Dempsey.

"I'd like a little farm where I can rest and grow a few things for my needs," replied Tate.

"It's yours, Bill," Dempsey replied. "I'll be gone for two or three weeks. You get yourself the farm and set it up. How much do you think it will cost?"

"About $10,000," answered Bill.

"I expect you to have everything ready when I return. I won't be gone for long. I'll close the deal for you to mortgage the farm to me."

Bill Tate was happy that day. He left Jack with a grin and a hefty handshake. Dempsey's offer to help had brought hope to Tate.

About four weeks later Dempsey returned to Chicago for an engagement. His first move was to contact Tate. He went to the Morrison Hotel and inquired of the boxing crowd where he could find his old trainer. The first person to greet Dempsey was Charley White, one of the nation's leading lightweights.

"You're too late, Jack," White said. "Tate was buried about ten days ago. He died of a heart attack."

Percy Thompson, a friend of Tate's, turned to Dempsey and said, "Don't worry, Bill died happy, because his friend Jack Dempsey hadn't let him down."

Dempsey was a sucker when it came to dealing out loans, nearly all of which were never returned. While on one of his refereeing tours, Jack was hired by Bobby Mansfield, a Southern promoter, to referee a boxing match in Monroe, Louisiana. When the bout was over, Jack said to Mansfield that if he ever required any help, he was to call upon the Manassa Mauler.

This was one time when Dempsey's aid worked highly in his favor. A few months passed and Dempsey received a wire from the promoter requesting financial aid:

> HAVE CHANCE TO BUY PROMISING OIL LEASE FOR $1,200. HAVE ONLY $800 AND TIME RUNNING OUT. CAN YOU HELP?

The telegram came from East Texas, Texas, as a result of which Mansfield's name didn't register with Dempsey. However, Jack took a gamble and wired the money.

Four months later, Dempsey received a wire from Mansfield:

> WE'VE HIT THE JACKPOT. HIT OIL. LOOKING AFTER YOUR SHARE. COME DOWN.

In relating the story, Jack said that his generosity had paid off well.

"I received a fine payment for my small investment. The gamble paid off for all concerned."

In 1939, the night before Jack was rushed to a hospital to undergo an appendix operation that nearly snuffed out his life, I asked him what was his toughest encounter since his retirement.

"Are you kidding," he replied, "keeping my temper."

"From whom?" I asked.

"From wiseacres who make a pass at me when they come in to greet me. I get a kick out of their visit but not the passes which apparently go with the satisfaction or notoriety, so that when they get back home, they can tell the folks about it."

"How do you avoid from striking back," I inquired.

"By keeping my hands in my pocket and remaining a few feet away."

The uncertainty of the past, the care with which he speaks, have given way to a far more refined man—a new Dempsey who arose from a roaming life in the West, a Dempsey who no longer shifts about when confronting persons of high education, men of power. The fidgety Jack Dempsey is gone—the more cultivated Dempsey is now in evidence.

There are many events in Dempsey's career one cannot forget. The destruction of Luis Angel Firpo, the Wild Bull of the Pampas, is but one, itself an indelible ring epic.

Much less publicized but sometimes nearly as unforgettable were the incidents in Dempsey's training camps. What reporter will ever forget the Toledo, Shelby, and Saratoga Springs layouts, where reams of material for daily yarns were garnered! Those colorful camps were ideal setups for boxing writers.

On one occasion Jim Johnson, a sparmate, made the mistake of tossing a haymaker that struck Jack's jaw and stunned him. The Manassa Mauler, dazed, shaking his head, suddenly regained his equilibrium and landed a shot that came up from the mat and sent his sparmate spinning across the ring into the ropes.

As he watched his sparmate wiping the bloody nose and mouth after he was dragged to his corner, Dempsey remarked, "Well, he asked for it. He was trying to show me up, wasn't he? He'll know better next time."

Training for his second fight with Gunboat Smith, Jack sparred with Clay Turner one afternoon. Clay kept prancing around the ring. Dempsey was visibly upset. He did land a few good punches to Turner's body, but he expected more action and became annoyed.

"Don't keep running away. I've got you here to help me get into fighting trim. I'm trying to get into condition. Make a stand," Dempsey ordered.

Turner did. He made one stab, missing as Jack turned his head to one side. Dempsey then let go a right, straight as an arrow. It crashed against his sparmate's jaw with a thud. Turner landed on the canvas with two of his upper teeth resting alongside him.

"Sorry, pal," remarked Jack. "It's all in the game."

His sparmates often complained about the rough treatment they received in the daily workouts, but Jack's ready answer was: "Well, they're well paid, aren't they? If they make good, they often are given a spot on the preliminary card."

30

"BOXING IS A GREAT SPORT," Dempsey opines. "It must be to have survived so many vicious attacks over the years.

"World War I produced a number of greats in all divisions. Many good boxers came out of that conflict. We had more clubs in New York than ever before and boxing thrived. But today there are a number of factors that have set boxing back.

"What the sport lacks today is the independent promoter," continued Jack. "When one considers that New York City, the boxing center for many years, has only three regular clubs, two owned by Madison Square Garden, he can readily understand the fall of pugilism in the Empire State. The independent promoter has closed shop. He cannot continue without the aid of television and that is closed to him.

"The situation is serious. It demands the attention of boxing commissions not only in New York but in all states.

"Somewhere in our country and in Canada there must be capable boxing material, but I fear that while the Vietnam War is on, there will be little development of new talent. Once we locate the material, with proper training, we can develop fighters such as we had following World War I and for a short time after World War II.

"I believe we'll develop good talent, a worthwhile crop after the Vietnam War has ended."

Since the 1920s, boxing has undergone many changes. And when one compares the contemporary scene with that of Dempsey's heyday and thereafter, there is often the temptation to despair.

Speaking of his own era, Dempsey recalls, "It was an era in boxing that saw the rise of a flock of talented pugilists who brought boxing to the heights. When I was champion and for several years following my defeats at the hands of Tunney, my excellent successor, fellows like Johnny Dundee, Harry Greb, Joe Louis, among others, kept the sport in the spotlight with thrilling, rip-roaring contests. There were clever fights in which Tommy Loughran, a master technician, figured. And Willie Pep, a dynamic youngster, and Billy Petrolle, to name a couple, could always keep the pot boiling."

Dempsey has always kept abreast of the boxing situation in every division. He believes the health of the whole sport depends on the abilities of the participants in each division, not just in the heavy class. He delights in noting the excellent talent the lightweight division has produced over the years. "Some of our greatest attractions came from that class," said Jack.

"Remember the thrilling contests in which Barney Ross, Tony Canzoneri, Jimmy McLarnin, and Petrolle, to name just a few, appeared?" asked Dempsey, nostalgically. "They fought at a time when the heavyweights, with Louis on top, were making ring history. Yet there was as much interest in the fights of the lower classifications as there was in the top two classes. That's what kept boxing alive in those days.

"Who among us who saw Petrolle at the height of his career can forget the thrillers in which he engaged? Or those of Ross, McLarnin, Pancho Villa, and Mickey Walker? We may not have the stars of the old days available, but if we had more fight clubs, we could develop talent to keep the sport at a high level.

"True, times have changed," continued Jack. "We can no longer count on the magnetism of sockers like Louis and Marciano, and ring artists like Billy Conn, Lou Ambers, and Canzoneri to give us the thrills that pack a stadium. But what we have is what we must work with.

"In my opinion, there are many youngsters eager to be given the opportunity to make good in boxing. Unfortunately, however, there is a dearth of boxing organizations and clubs.

"It is an unhealthy situation, one that, in my opinion, can be cured only through government control of the sport, something I have urged for several years. Given the opportunity and encouragement, the kids can bring the sport back to where it belongs."

Dempsey can make a most convincing case in behalf of his views on remedying the present plight of boxing. In addition to having more clubs, Jack believes beginners should have more pay, at least more than they receive in the smaller clubs. Too, new talent should be fighting more four-rounders. Too many promoters, says Dempsey, kill the advance of the young talent by pitting them against opponents in ten-round bouts when they are not ready for contests of that length.

"They should be learning their trade in four-round bouts," insists Jack. "Under such a program they could engage in more matches. Giving the beginners a pittance doesn't help the buildup of new talent. A youngster competing in a four-rounder should get at least $50. It costs money be a fighter. License fees, gym dues, doctors' fees for special examinations—all these, plus other things, work a hardship on the kids.

"When I entered the pro field, I had quite a number of four-round bouts, many of which are not listed in my record. They were usually tough ones, but they prepared me for the contest that led to my championship match with Willard. My experience fighting four-rounders helped me plenty in my fight with Jess. I started punching from the opening gong. I attribute my success largely to the many bouts I had in the four-round sector."

During our discussion, I asked Dempsey what made his era so different from the boxing scene today.

"The arenas in which we fought, the people who came to see the fights, the locale in which the fight was staged—everything, in fact. It was all so different from what we have today. The picturesqueness cannot be erased from your memory. The stories of the old ring battles are never-to-be-forgotten tales," said Jack, with fondness.

"Sure, we didn't have cushion-covered chairs, the ushers with their pressed uniforms, the ring guarded by special police. But we had the thoroughbred fans, men whose presence and enthusiasm urged us to go all out."

Listening to Dempsey's reminiscences, one can easily understand why those who are attempting to clean up boxing today stand aces high with the ex-champ. Jack himself has made appearances before legislative bodies and given talks before public-spirited citizens in behalf of bettering the fight scene. He seldom misses an opportunity to bring to the attention of the public the necessity of keeping the sport on a high level.

Zeroing in on the unsavory sorts, Dempsey declares that state athletic commissions have "permitted incompetent persons to take over the management of beginners. One type of incompetent is the joker who treats boxing as a toy; the other treats it as a tool. The first invests some money in a promising lad, but soon discards him when he finds the gamble too risky due to the lengthy period it takes to get into the big-money class. The second type is not interested in the advancement of the sport. Ethics play no part in the management. If a boy is brought along too rapidly, is overmatched and loses, the manager discards him. I've seen a lot of that over the years."

As sad a condition as that is the loss of the small clubs. At one time they flooded the land. New York State, for example, onetime leader of the nation in this area, once had 34 clubs. It now has three. For this, says Dempsey, the athletic commission of that state must take the blame.

"Like it or not," says Dempsey, "local arenas are the only places left where an enthusiastic kid who has his eyes focused on a fight future can make any headway and learn the ropes. Even these we no longer have in New York. California is the pacesetter. The majority of the good talent developed in the past few years has come from the Pacific Coast.

"Government control would help, but our lawmakers in Washington have little or no desire to enter the boxing field.

There's nothing more I'd like to see than boxing placed under government control. It would be the means of obtaining a national revival of interest, an aid to cities, states, and government."

Specifically, this control should take the form of a national boxing commission. Ever since his retirement as a boxing and wrestling referee, Jack has campaigned for a national commission as the best means of protecting the interests of pugilism. Twice he has pleaded his case in our nation's capital, pointing out boxing's illnesses and how to cure them. However, nothing was accomplished.

Several congressmen listened to Jack's plea, which was aided by the testimony of others, among whom were Gene Tunney, Abe Greene (the World Boxing Association's commissioner), and I. The matter was then shelved for another meeting, which never materialized.

My personal opinion is that Dempsey would make an excellent chairman of a national boxing commission. If such a commission were appointed with Jack as its head, it is safe to predict that Dempsey would soon be rid of the hangers-on, the unsavory characters who bleed the poor boxers they control. Unfortunately, most such managers operate secretly behind the protection of gangsters, and the law as it now reads cannot get at them.

"I hope that we will see the day when our government will organize a national commission that will bring boxing into the spotlight again, as it was when I was a member of the fistic brigade," mused Dempsey. "The vast sums obtained by our government, New York State, and other states where the Frazier-Clay contest was shown, illustrate the heights boxing occupies as a major sports interest."

Testimony to Jack's various endeavors in behalf of boxing is plentiful. On December 11, 1957, Dempsey received the annual James J. Walker Memorial Award from the New York Boxing Writers' Association, for long and meritorious service to the sport. Previously, in 1938, Jack was the recipient of the Edward J. Neil Trophy, an honor bestowed on the one who has done the most for boxing during the previous year.

31

Jack Dempsey and Joe Louis. These are the names that most frequently crop up when the talk turns to boxing. They afford a startling contrast in disposition and personal habits, though they are almost alike to the average fight fan. They were tops in their division at the height of their careers; both had a magic hold on the public; each desired to give all who were qualified to fight for the crown an opportunity to compete for it; neither ever lost his head because of public flattery.

These aside, their differences form an interesting contrast. Dempsey was cordial and loved to mingle with the common folk. He genuinely enjoyed the admiration of the throng and endeared himself to the public in a lasting way.

When Jack appears on television, those in the studio and those who watch him on the screen find him the same congenial, soft-spoken "champ," as he still is called. He can hold an audience with his stories about fights and fighters and about the current situation in world boxing, far more easily than most other former pugilists. He has the knack of bringing home the points in a convincing manner—no stalling, no hesitation, no beating-around-the-bush tactics. And he is cordiality personified.

Louis, for the greater part of his fighting career and even after his retirement, was cold to public acclaim. He preferred to avoid crowds. Joe's ring battles, with the exception of his second Schmeling contest, were fought calmly. He was an iceberg when he faced his opponent; one of the coldest champions I've known.

The only time I saw a change in him and in his method of attack was when he clashed with Max Schmeling in 1938 in their second engagement. His usual nonchalance was gone. Joe was out for revenge for the knockout he suffered in their June 1936 encounter and he blazed away with flailing fists from the first sound of the gong.

Like Louis, Dempsey and Marciano were great punchers. But neither Dempsey nor Marciano ever numbed an opponent into defeat as did the Brown Bomber when he fought Schmeling the second time.

Dempsey, with the speed of an unleashed tiger, combined with his bobbing and weaving style, would have outgeneraled Louis, in my opinion. Accustomed to a stand-up target, Joe would have been at sea against the style of Dempsey. That was proven in his fight with Arturo Godoy, in which Godoy lasted 15 rounds, and again in his bout with Jersey Joe Walcott, in which fast footwork and a crouch made Louis almost helpless.

In all of Louis's fights, he displayed none too robust a chin, being dropped to the canvas several times. Those knockdowns, if nothing else, would be sufficient cause for placing Dempsey on top in a dream battle between them. No wild-swinging Galento, no light-hitting Buddy Baer would have dropped Dempsey as they did Louis.

When Louis entered the ring, he was a picture of serenity. When listening to the referee's instructions, he was the calmest man in the arena.

Dempsey, however, was of a most excitable nature once he got into the ring with an opponent. Jack was a man on fire while awaiting the call to arms. Listening to instructions, he never eyed his opponent or the official. He kept his eyes glued to the canvas. His body was tense, lusting for the action soon to follow. And once the bell clanged, he became a tiger man.

Unleashed, Manassa Jack burned up his energy in the first few rounds in his eagerness to connect with a haymaker. He was always out to end the fight as quickly as possible.

Louis, on the other hand, could wait it out for many rounds until such time as he spotted an opening to land the punch soporific. That's why those who favor Dempsey over the Brown Bomber in a dream battle are confident the Manassa Mauler would early have caught Louis with a blow that would have ended the fray.

There are those who argue that Louis would have whipped Dempsey because, under present rules, Jack would not have been permitted to stand over his fallen opponent as happened in many of his battles—especially the Willard, Firpo, and Brennan contests—and batter his rival to the canvas again as quickly as he rose from the ring floor.

Unlike Louis, who was a strict observer of the rules, Dempsey could not have allowed himself to be cramped by the niceties of ring behavior once he decked his opponent. Had he fought in the present era the way he did against most of his opponents, particularly Big Jess and Firpo, in all probability Jack would have faced disqualification.

In the fight with Willard, Manassa Jack was at his best. Never before or after did he show quite the same fighting form, the tear-in, energetic style, the killer instinct, which he exhibited in the Toledo battle.

The Louis-Schmeling return engagement was the Brown Bomber's best. He displayed in that contest many of the fighting assets possessed by Dempsey. But even in that hectic affair, Joe failed to exhibit the fighting form displayed by Manassa Jack against Big Jess. A dream fight between Joe and Jack, with each in the fighting trim displayed in the two battles mentioned, would have treated the fans to an all-time thriller.

Who would have won? I pick Dempsey. That also was the vote of most of the servicemen whom I visited in camps and hospitals during World War II. After I had shown the pictures of the Dempsey-Willard battle, Louis vs. Schmeling, and Louis vs. Billy Conn, and after discussion of what they had just seen—the fighters' styles, their hitting power, their ability to absorb punishment—the vote was nearly always overwhelmingly in favor of Dempsey. In some hospitals or camps, there were as many as 500 servicemen in attendance.

Dempsey demonstrated in all his fights that he could withstand a healthy wallop to the jaw more readily than could Louis, who was vulnerable to such an attack. The Manassa Mauler could both deliver and take a good punch.

When one considers the number of times Louis was down in fights—nine in all—I doubt that a Dempsey-Louis contest would have gone beyond ten rounds when Manassa Jack was in his prime.

Braddock, Schmeling, Buddy Baer, Tony Galento, Marciano, and Walcott each dropped the Brown Bomber. Having seen both Jack and Joe in almost all of their major contests, I venture that the Dempsey who battered Willard was the master of all his successors and top contenders.

Thus, in a Dempsey-Louis match, I cast my ballot for Dempsey. The speed of the Manassa Mauler, his killer instinct, his ability to take heavy punches, his steady attack—all of these would have combined to accomplish what Jack did against Willard, though probably less quickly.

The fighter who scored the first solid punch to the jaw in such a contest would have won the fight. That man, I think, would have been Dempsey. He would have proved too fast on the attack for the Brown Bomber.

Many critics point to the fight with Tom Gibbons that went the limit of 15 rounds. They ask what chance would Dempsey have had that day against a heavy hitter like Louis.

The comparison must be made at the time when Louis and Jack were at the height of their careers. When Dempsey fought Gibbons, he had to face a number of hazards that affected his fighting form.

The critics also fail to take into consideration the Louis–Tommy Farr battle of 1937, in which the Welshman went the limit with the Bomber. The following year Farr fought Braddock, Max Baer, and Lou Nova. In January 1939 he faced Red Burman. Farr lost every one of those fights. Farr would never have gone 15 rounds with Manassa Jack when the latter was in his prime.

If Dempsey had been at the height of his career during the

present TV era, he would have reaped twice the fortune he gained in his ring battles, a fortune which, as it was, reached into the millions. Much of it was lost during the depression days, however. No fighter, past or present, could have commanded the attention of a television audience the way the Dempsey of the Willard, Carpentier, and Firpo battles could have.

Next to Jack come Louis and Marciano as tremendous TV magnets.

Late in 1970, when the new Madison Square Garden was starting a Hall of Fame for boxing, Dempsey was chosen top man of the six named. Manassa Jack edged Louis 44 to 43, with Sugar Ray Robinson third. Then followed Benny Leonard, Marciano, and Henry Armstrong. The six joined greats of other sports—88 selections in all—for the Garden exhibit.

Jimmy DeForest, famous trainer, following the Firpo-Dempsey fight, was asked to write a special story on the thriller for me for the *New York Press.* Here is part of the article:

"I've been a trainer all my life. I've handled Dempsey in several fights and I'm not prejudiced; but frankly, I get tired telling readers that, in my opinion, the top heavyweight over the years is Jack Dempsey. He is the greatest.

"For personality, I'll stand by John L. Sullivan. I regard him as the most popular in our boxing history. His big voice, boisterous laugh, quality of good fellowship, generosity, in both time and money, made him a heavy winner.

"But as a fighting man, the Great John L., in his best days, would have gone down before a Dempsey assault such as Jack threw at Willard. I believe that none of the crop that came up from Sullivan to Willard would have beaten Dempsey.

"Jack Johnson is the one heavyweight who might have had a chance. But, by the time Dempsey had become champion, Johnson's loose living made him too much of a target for a hitter like Dempsey. Agility also would have played a big part in Dempsey's favor."

There was an occasion when Jimmy Braddock was invited to be the guest speaker at an Elks' Sports Night. He was asked whether Dempsey was a harder slugger than Marciano.

He told the enthusiastic turnout that he would hand Jack the honors.

"Marciano was a harder puncher than Joe Louis," Braddock said, "but I think the top man as a hitter among the heavyweights of my time was Jack Dempsey. Rocky would hurt you more with a single punch than would Louis. Dempsey, though, was a rough, tough heavyweight, a terrific hitter, quicker than either Joe or Rocky with his fists. That's why I favor Dempsey over all other heavyweights of my time."

In the majority of the interviews I've conducted, I've found Braddock's opinion of Dempsey upheld. Dempsey has come out leading the top men by a fair margin. Jeffries, Marciano, Tunney, Johnson, Louis get their share of the votes, but Dempsey invariably leads the field.

One of my interviews was with Jeffries, a great power puncher, in 1952 in his California home.

"I met the toughest in my day," Jim told me. "They were wonderful hitters. Unfortunately, it is difficult to make comparisons of fighters of different periods.

"I followed Dempsey's rise to fame, saw him fight only three times, but what I saw convinces me that he would have emerged the winner over Fitzsimmons, Corbett, and Johnson. He was rugged, tough, quick, a power hitter with strong arms and shoulders. He was fast and punched well. With those assets I believe he stood out as one of the great heavyweights of all time."

I told Jeffries that a number of leading sportswriters were of the opinion that Dempsey tried to dispose of his opponents early because he couldn't go beyond 15 rounds.

"That's ridiculous!" Jeffries replied. "A fighter is aware of the number of rounds for which the bout is arranged and trains accordingly. The training is different for a combat of 25 rounds than it would be for 15 or 20 rounds. I'm sure Dempsey took that into consideration when he started his training routine.

"I suppose many experts imagined that Dempsey couldn't go

the longer route. I fought only five bouts at 20 rounds or more and one at 15. All others ended quickly. Twenty-five rounds were the limit in my day; 15 is tops now.

"Well, I always tried to put my man away before those limits were reached. I had to train for a 25-round fight because my fight might go that number. Dempsey never had to train for any bouts beyond 15.

"Dempsey, at the height of his career, would not have had much to fear from the men I fought. His punching ability and aggressiveness would have been to his great advantage."

Coming from one of the outstanding heavyweights of all time, that was an extreme compliment.

"I've read so much about Jeffries, yet I never saw him in action. I wish I had seen him," said Dempsey, when I told him about what the Boilermaker had said.

Charley Harvey, one of the most outstanding of all managers, a man responsible for bringing to America Jimmy Wilde, Len Harvey, and Ted Kid Lewis, among other famous Britishers, joined in the Dempsey accolade. A few months before he died, I interviewed Charley.

"I have seen every great heavyweight in modern ring history," he said. "I saw John L. Sullivan fight Herbert Slade, Tug Wilson, and Charley Mitchell. I saw Peter Jackson in his greatest battles. I watched Bob Fitzsimmons, Jim Corbett, Jim Jeffries, and Jess Willard in their major competition.

"Two boxers stand out in my opinion on an equal basis—the great John L. Sullivan and Jack Dempsey. Dempsey stands high in my esteem. Sullivan has been my idol over the years. There were many points of similarity in their styles.

"John L. was a rushing, tearing-in, two-fisted fighter with a power punch. He was big, fast, and courageous.

"Dempsey too was a rushing, tear-in fighter, carrying a finishing punch in either fist. I saw the greatest heavyweights in over 50 years of association with boxing, but I doubt that the ring ever produced a more effective battler than the man I saw tear into Willard and batter him into a helpless state.

"The manner in which Dempsey destroyed the Pottawatomie Giant made me hark back to the days of Sullivan. With all due respect to the crashing power of the Boston Strong Boy, I doubt he could have done the job on Willard with the neatness and dispatch exhibited by Dempsey.

"What I liked about Dempsey was the speed with which he opened an attack. It seemed to me that he always was eager to get it over with as quickly as possible. He wasted little time."

I once met Battling Nelson, the old lightweight champ, at the Bismarck Hotel in Chicago. He had seen Jack's fight with Willard and was spending a few days in the Windy City seeking a vaudeville engagement. While sitting at a lunch counter, I asked him what he thought of the new heavyweight champion.

"What's in it for me if I tell you," he replied.

"Fifty bucks," I said, "and a meal with me."

Nelson quickly accepted.

"All I've been hearing since I came here two nights ago is what Sullivan, Corbett, Fitzsimmons, and Jeffries would have done to Dempsey," said Bat. "There never was a fighter who could have brought Willard down the way Dempsey did. Jack is fast, clever, and a terrific puncher.

"I never saw Sullivan fight, but I believe that Dempsey would have been too strong for him. Corbett, I think, would have been a softer touch for Jack. Dempsey would have made Fitz look like a prisoner with two iron balls chained to his feet. In Dempsey I saw the most punishing fighter the heavies have produced.

"They say that Jack Johnson would have stopped Dempsey. Well, Johnson was clever and a good-punching heavyweight, but I think that Dempsey would have been too shifty for him.

"As for Marvin Hart, Tommy Burns, and Jim Jeffries, I'm certain that Dempsey would have whipped the first two but would have had a tough time with Jeffries. That bout would have been a close one."

James J. (Sunny Jim) Coffroth, famed West Coast promoter of the old days, visited New York and came to see me one day in the sports department of the *New York Press.* We were discussing boxing in general; since Dempsey was appearing on the Pacific Coast, I asked Jim if he had seen Dempsey fight.

"Yes," he replied, "and he looks good. He's a heavy hitter and fearless. I think he'll come along brilliantly. Wish I had him."

A few years later when Rickard started promoting in New York, Coffroth visited the city again. By now Dempsey was Tex's major attraction. Coffroth, a good friend of Kearns', had come to New York at the manager's invitation to see Manassa Jack fight Firpo. After the knockout of the Wild Bull, I interviewed Coffroth again.

"Jim, what's your opinion of Dempsey now?" I asked. You've seen all the past masters. Does he remind you of one in particular?"

"Well, what he did to Willard and now to the Argentinian makes me feel that I've seen a second Terry McGovern, a master of destruction. Jack is a ferocious fellow, as was Terry. He has a great fighting heart.

"Every round seems to be the last with him. I've heard some of my friends say that he wouldn't have gone 20 rounds with some of the tough ones in my time as a promoter. Well, we had a lot of them, but Dempsey would have held his own with any.

"I don't like to compare fighters, but when I saw Jack take Willard apart and now maul Firpo, I wonder what a Dempsey-Jeffries bout would have been! In all my career I've never seen fighters show such ferocity as that which Dempsey hurled at Willard and Firpo."

In 1950, Jack, in a national poll conducted by the Associated Press, was voted The Fighter of the Half-Century.

And on June 7, 1965, at a meeting of the Academy of Sports Editors in Boston, Dempsey was selected the king of all heavyweights. Of the 100 sports editors who participated, 90 percent voted for the Manassa Mauler. Joe Louis was next with 82 percent, and Gene Tunney placed third with 60. Rocky Marciano captured 50 percent for fourth place.

Following were Jack Johnson with 47 percent; James J. Corbett, 40; James J. Jeffries, 36; John L. Sullivan, 35; Bob Fitzsimmons, 23; and Jess Willard, 10.

In every selection of the ten greatest heavyweights in modern times, Dempsey's name is always in the top five. In most, he is listed number one.

Encomiums to Dempsey the fighter are legion. But one of the

most memorable of all tributes was paid not to Dempsey the fighter but to Dempsey the man. When asked who was the greatest gentleman he knew in sports, the esteemed Grantland Rice replied:

"There's only one, Jack Dempsey. There is no one to compare with him."

There's a happy footnote to Jack's being voted The Fighter of the Half-Century. It provided the occasion for the reunion of Dempsey and his old manager, Jack Kearns.

Both Jacks were guests of honor at a dinner in New York's Hotel Edison where Dempsey received the coveted Fighter of the Half-Century Award. This was the first time since 1926, when they openly broke their partnership, that Dempsey and Kearns had attended the same function. Now, 24 years later, they nodded, then spoke casually for a few minutes. Shortly after, Dempsey was called upon for a speech.

He looked about the dais, greeted some friends, tapped the podium as one who is uncertain of what to say, then remarked:

"I'm happy to be here as a guest. Many years have elapsed since Jack Kearns and I appeared at a function like this. Every fighter owes something to his manager, the man who brought him to the front. I had a number of managers, but I didn't find the right one until I teamed up with Jack Kearns, and I'm happy to be here with him again and tell him so."

A roar of applause followed. Tears rolled down the cheeks of Kearns, whose astonishment at the words of his former prize boxer was an emotional experience not soon to be forgotten by the old pilot.

Dempsey looked down on Kearns with a smile. Then Manassa Jack continued:

"He told me I was the greatest puncher in the world and I believed him. I'll always be grateful to him for making me a world champion.

"He instilled confidence in me as no other manager could have done. It was Jack Kearns who enabled me to win the world heavyweight championship and to become a wealthy man, an honored citizen. For that I thank him."

32

In 1936, Joe Louis had been kayoed by Max Schmeling. The return bout was set for June 22, 1938, at the Yankee Stadium in New York. As the showdown time approached, interest mounted. One of those avidly interested was Jack Dempsey.

Louis, out to avenge his 12th-round knockout at the hands of the German, had commenced his training for the return engagement. One day Hype Igoe of the *New York Journal,* Murray Lewin of the *Daily Mirror,* Jimmy Dawson of the *New York Times,* Dempsey, and I decided to see one of the Brown Bomber's workouts. On the way to the camp, Igoe coaxed Dempsey into giving Joe a few pointers on how to tackle Schmeling.

"Joe must beat him," said Hype, "and you, Jack, must show him how."

Dempsey agreed. During the trip to the camp Jack outlined what he would do if he himself were in Louis's shoes.

We were certain that Louis and his trainer, Jack Blackburn, would have no objection to Hype's plan.

On arriving Hype first discussed the matter with Blackburn.

He told the trainer that Dempsey had watched Joe several times. As a result, Jack had made numerous observations which he felt certain would help Louis defeat Schmeling.

Blackburn listened and had no objection.

"Joe will be happy to listen to you, Jack," he told Dempsey.

Into Louis's room we all went. We were greeted with a smile and a handshake by Joe, who seemed very happy to see Dempsey.

"Joe, you've got to give it everything you've got in the first minute of the opening round," Dempsey advised Louis.

Then Jack outlined how he would fight the German, while Blackburn kept nodding approval.

"Schmeling is a slow starter," said Dempsey. "He takes time out to think. I've seen you do the same, Joe. Don't do that. Turn on the juice as soon as you face your man. Give him no time to get set. You can do it, Joe.

"We've got to keep that title in our country and it's up to you to do it. You can do it better than anyone else, Joe. If he wins, the title will be in Hitler's hands and it will take a long time before we get it back, Joe."

So ended Jack's admonition. It was serious advice to the man who held the world heavyweight title. Blackburn agreed with what Jack had said.

"You've got something there, Jack," said Louis's trainer, a great fighter in his day. "I'm sure Joe understands."

When the fight was over, Dempsey and Igoe were elated. The title remained in our country by virtue of one of the quickest knockouts in ring history among the heavyweights.

Schmeling's knockout of Louis in their first bout had left its mark on the Brown Bomber, a stigma he couldn't forget. Now he had avenged that mark on his record.

The day after the fight, while meeting the press, Joe told of the meeting and how Jack's visit had bolstered him. It gave him the added incentive to put Schmeling away.

Although the excellent training sessions conducted by Blackburn got Louis into the wonderful condition he displayed, there could be no doubt that the visit of Dempsey had its influence on the Brown Bomber.

33

CHAMPION JACK DEMPSEY had wonderful shoulder development. In telling how he developed his power punch, Dempsey said that he never knew until after he had fought Willard the difference between biceps and triceps. He thought that if the upper part of the body was muscular, that was all one required in the development of the knockout punch.

"But I learned after I had defeated Willard that I was wrong," mused Dempsey. "I learned that to achieve my knockout ambition it was necessary for me to develop all parts of my body, and I set out to do that.

"The hard work I did when I was a youngster helped me to attain my aim when I grew older. As soon as I was old enough to wear boxing gloves, I was put to work. Years of it made me a fighting man. No allowance was made for my youth. I hired out to do a man's job although I was only a boy, and I did it. That farm work was the best thing that ever happened to me. It helped me to develop my arms, shoulders, and back—physical growth that put me in trim for the arduous work I later encountered when I entered the ring.

"The grimy, dirty work in the copper mines in my later period of development, performed many feet underground—hauling, lifting, swinging a pick—helped in the buildup. All that manual labor counted in my favor."

I asked Jack if the tough punches he took before he joined the professional fighting ranks didn't discourage him.

"No, I had good arms and wonderful hands and I used them to advantage in my early bouts. Even in those fights, I carried a good wallop in either fist. That is what made me decide on a pro fighting career. I got the impression that in my punching power, I had special assets."

Jack also attributes his remarkable punching power to big bones, a well-developed wrist, a squareness across the knuckles, and strength in the striking muscles of the upper arm, shoulders, and back.

While explaining the necessity of these properties to a fighter, Dempsey suddenly added, "We left something out—the faculty of proper leverage must also be considered."

If Dempsey had any punches that might be termed his aces, they were his terrific left to the body and right to the jaw, which generally were delivered with a one-two effect. He also delivered a good left hook to the head and a righthand drive to the heart. These were very noticeable in his fight with Willard.

The opinion of most analysts of Dempsey's career is that Jack was merely a rough, tough slugger with power behind his punches. His critics fail to recognize that he possessed ring science and cleverness above those of the average fighter.

Tough and rugged he was, to be sure, but those who fought him often remarked that Jack had a fighting head and ranked well up in other ring qualities, especially in versatility and power hitting. His animallike ring movements and hitting power were the difference when Dempsey floored Willard seven times with clouts on the jaw. Jack Dempsey at his best was the Thor of the Ring.

Although Dempsey was one of the hardest hitters of modern times, he admits having been scared frequently. "Only a sucker or an idiot would profess himself to be absolutely fearless. The average fighter gets goose pimples when he's in a tight squeeze, but if he is a good fighter, he usually battles his way out of the situation," said Jack. "I've faced times when I had plenty to worry me, and on occasions, I've been in danger of my life, but I overcame the fear.

"Every time I got into the ring, I was nervous. The way I looked at it, I figured that a fighter lacked ambition if he went into the ring calm and contented. That is why in all my major bouts, except the Gibbons contest, I went all out in an attempt to end the fight as quickly as possible. I think I also lacked that incentive in the first fight with Gene Tunney, due to my difficulties with Jack Kearns."

What was Dempsey's general feeling when facing an opponent?

"I suppose the same as that possessed by any other fighter. I always went out to win as quickly as I could, but don't recall ever carrying enmity into the ring with me. I regarded the men I faced simply as opponents—nothing more or less. We each had a job to perform and I know I always did it the best way I could," said Dempsey.

I asked Jack what are the requisites for a top fighter and he replied:

"A good fighter must have many qualities. First comes top physical condition. No fighter should enter into ring combat unless he knows he is physically fit. He must be able to take and give a good punch. Speed is another essential. He should be able to work rapidly with his hands and be able to move about in a position from which he can both strike and avoid being hit.

"He must like to fight. Keeping his weight within the requirements of his class is also essential. If one is a heavyweight, weight doesn't count so much as in other divisions, so long as one doesn't become flabby and slow down.

"A top heavyweight should possess speed, punching power, plus the ability to take a good punch. Slow-moving fighters are useless. They can make no progress. They are impeded by their movements," he concluded.

34

IT WAS March 8, 1971. The Madison Square Garden clock registered 10:30 P.M. It was time to start the Clay-Frazier fight. Johnny Addie had introduced the celebrities, but one famous boxer of past years had been forgotten—Jack Dempsey.

From the spectators came a huge clamor for Dempsey to enter the ring. "We want Dempsey," chanted the galleryites.

Addie quickly took notice of his failure. "Jack Dempsey," Addie called, "please come into the ring."

The huge gathering, almost to a man, stood and applauded as Dempsey walked from his seat, grasped the ring ropes, and entered. An ovation such as few others have ever received in the famed arena followed. Jack smiled, shook hands with the boxers in their respective corners, and left the ring.

When the fight was over, I asked Dempsey for his opinion of the decision, which had been awarded to Frazier. Jack was diplomatic. He didn't want to be placed in an awkward position.

"It was a fine fight," he said. "I leave the decision to those assigned to handle the fight. I never like to comment on such matters. I always remember the fight in Chicago with Tunney. Whatever I might say will be expanded, and if it's contrary to the official verdict, it will be the subject of controversy, which hurts the game. I learned that during my term as heavyweight champion. The best way to help the sport is not to discuss such matters, especially if you are in the public spotlight."

Asked to comment on the ability of Frazier as compared with that of others, all Jack would say was:

"He's the best man in the division as of now. Let it go at that. There is plenty of time to rank him with other champions after he retires. He did a good job tonight. Let it stand at that."

Walking with him after the fight, I asked about the current leaders in the heavyweight division. How would Frazier, Clay, and other top-rated pugilists have fared against the majority of the men Jack had fought?

"You know we are living in a period different from that in which Tunney, Willard, Firpo, Carpentier, among others, were tops. Many changes have taken place in the boxing world. Those who are the leaders today have earned their posts just as those who fought in my time earned their prestige.

"What confronts the fight fans today is the best he can see. Frazier is a tough boy. He's always at his man.

"Clay is a clever boxer, one of the best in recent years. Unfortunately for him, his long layoff lowered his fighting qualities. At this stage, he reminds me of myself in the first fight with Tunney, when I quickly learned what it means to be rusty. Much of the fine speed Clay displayed in all his fights prior to retiring temporarily, had left him. Three years of ring rustiness take their toll.

"There are plenty of good boxers in our country. Unfortunately they aren't kept busy. Blame that on the shortage of fight clubs."

35

In these turbulent days, Jack Dempsey, now 77, leads a quiet life, or as quiet a life as one still so much in the public eye can lead.

"My life is uneventful and happy," says Jack. "I no longer keep very close to the fight business, but I know who is around and I have my ideas about what goes on and who is doing what. I don't go to very many fights at Madison Square Garden but I try to keep pace with the heavyweights.

"One of my pet peeves still concerns fight judges. I favor the British system, which makes the referee boss of the bout and the decision. Judges usually confuse the issue. A good referee needs no help," maintains Dempsey.

Time was when Jack did a lot of refereeing around the country, but he hasn't been active in that respect for more than ten years.

"I got tired of the work," explains Jack, "though it was a good source of income. A big factor in my retirement from refereeing was my feeling that if I invaded an area, I was doing some local referee out of a good job."

Dempsey spends much of his time, though not quite as much as in previous years, at the Broadway restaurant that bears his name.

"How do I spend a typical day? Of course, that depends on where my wife, Deanna, and I happen to be.

"I get up around ten. We have breakfast at home, then I go to the market, shopping for things for the kitchen and the table.

"I usually arrive at the restaurant at twelve-thirty, the height of the luncheon business.

"Though Broadway is no longer what it used to be, we manage to do pretty well.

"On arrival at the restaurant I confer with the manager, the maitre d', and the head chef, all of whom are top men.

"Then begins one of the most interesting parts of my day. I am consulted, mostly by women, on every subject under the sun.

"They want to know about weight-watching, about diet and drinking, about sleeping and waking, about marriage and the single life. You would be amazed if you listened in.

"I try to be patient and considerate to everyone and give my opinions as I see them.

"I am asked many questions about boxing, of course—even by kindly old ladies from small towns. I am astonished at how much they know about fights and how much more they want to know.

"I talk and shake hands until about two-thirty, depending upon who is around. I get home around three and attend to family chores. I sometimes try to catch up on some reading, but still do not read very much. You remember how I spared my eyes during my ring days.

"After resting for a couple of hours, I am back at the restaurant for dinner. I get away sometimes for a show or movie and return to the restaurant around eleven. I spend about an hour there, then it's back to the apartment, and off to sleep and up around ten again. It's the same routine but I never tire of it.

"Some days, of course, there is an interlude. Deanna and I go off to the country or visit some friends. On weekends I don't go near the restaurant, as a rule.

"My trips to see my daughters and their families give me a big kick."

Jack's daughters, Barbara and Joan, have seven daughters between them. One daughter lives in Los Angeles, the other in suburban Van Nuys.

Dempsey has been married for 13 years to his fourth wife, the former Deanna Piatelli. They had been wed for 18 months before Jack made the announcement in August 1960.

When asked why the marriage was kept a secret for so long, Dempsey explained:

"It's no secret. My wife didn't want any publicity, that's all."

In a recent television appearance, Jack's lovely wife told the story of how they met. It seems that Deanna owned a jewelry shop in the lobby of the Hotel Manhattan in New York. "One day this big, handsome man brought in a broken cuff link to be repaired. I told him I did not do repair work," recalled Mrs. Dempsey.

" 'Can you tell me where to send it?' " he asked.

"I told him I did not know. He asked me to have a cup of coffee with him, but I refused. I had previously been aware that he had been watching me from the hotel balcony.

"I later learned that he had broken the cuff link on purpose as an excuse to come into the store. He told me his name was John L. Sullivan.

"When I told a girlfriend of mine about him, she laughed uproariously when I told her his name was John L. Sullivan.

"My friend explained that Sullivan was an oldtime champion who had been dead for many years and that the gentleman with the broken cuff link was none other than Jack Dempsey.

"Not having the faintest knowledge of boxing or sports, I asked, 'And who is Jack Dempsey?' I soon found out."

Of course, Jack and Deanna finally got together and were married in February 1959.

Deanna says of Jack: "What I love about him the most is his kindness. People need very much to be loved. Every day I tell my husband how much I love him."

The American public feels much the same way about the

ex-champ. The years away from the ring have not dulled his appeal. The glitter of Manhattan has left unsoiled the boyish charm of the man from Manassa.

True, the power punch is gone, but memory of it abides strong. As though it were yesterday, the eye can still behold the scowling form of Manassa Jack standing over his fallen foe. That fistic talent of old and his charisma and disarming radiance of today are enough to make Jack Dempsey one of the greatest sports figures ever to stride our land.

Dempsey and Hannah Williams, his third wife, at the Primo Carnera–Jack Sharkey title bout at Madison Square Garden Bowl, Long Island City, in June 1933.

Mine Host Dempsey does the honors with a salad at the opening of the restaurant that bears his name, in 1936. The other chef is Gus Hallitz.

Dempsey's eating establishment on Broadway and 49th Street, New York.

Manassa Jack takes the oath that made him a lieutenant commander in the U.S. Coast Guard in 1942. He receives the oath from Capt. G. U. Steward, commanding officer of the Manhattan Beach Training Station, Brooklyn.

The popular Dempsey referees a service bout while in the Coast Guard in World War II.

Dempsey shakes hands with Kearns in 1950 at boxing dinner in New York, after 24 years of estrangement. The champ was awarded a plaque as winner of the Associated Press poll for Fighter of the Half-Century.

Jack enjoying Christmas 1955 with daughter Joan (left), granddaughter Denise, daughter Barbara, and granddaughter Kim.

Appendix I

OFFICIAL RECORD OF DEMPSEY'S BIRTH

TOWN OF MANASSA

MANASSA, COLORADO

November
Tenth
1 9 2 5.

In Re: *Jack Dempsey*

Dear Sir:-

Your request for information regarding "Jack Dempsey" is received. I have looked up what information there is available to the clerk of the town of Manassa. To get the information you seem to be anxious to get, it was necessary for me to go to other records than those in the custody of the town Clerk.

The fees for this are one dollar which I take from your letter I may trust you to send me immediately on receipt of this information which I can certify to be correct.

"Jack Dempsey" the present world's heavyweight champion is the son of HYRUM DEMPSEY and Mary C. (Smoot) who are natives of West Virginia. The mother is a second cousin of the senior senator from Utah. His real name is WILLIAM HARRISON DEMPSEY, born in Manassa, Conejos County, Colorado on June 24th, 1895. His ancestry is native American as far as available records go.

It is said by some of the older settlers that there is some Indian blood in one of his parents, though this does not seem to be verified. His parents are of the Mormon faith—or were at one time—and "Jack" was supposed to be also in his younger days.

His present faith or creed I do not know. As to there being any change of name in the family, there does not seem to be any evidence of it. The name "Jack" is a "misnomer" or fighting name, his correct or legal name as stated above is William Harrison.

Yours very truly,

James A. Holman
Clerk and Recorder.

Appendix II

DEMPSEY'S FIGHT RECORD

(Early record unavailable. Started fighting in 1914 as Kid Blackie.)

1914

Date	Opponent	Result	Rounds
	Andy Malloy	L	10
Aug. 17	Young Herman, Ramona, Colo.	D	6

1915

Date	Opponent	Result	Rounds
Apr. 5	Jack Downey, Salt Lake City	L	4
Apr. 26	Anamas Campbell, Reno	KO	3
June 13	Johnny Sudenberg, Tonopah	W	10
July 3	Johnny Sudenberg, Goldfield	D	10
Dec. 13	Jack Downey, Salt Lake City	D	4
Dec. 20	Two Round Gillian, Salt Lake City	KO	1

Knockouts: Kid Hancock, 1; Billy Murphy, 1; Chief Gordon, 6; Johnny Person, 7; Joe Lions, 9; Fred Woods, 4; George Copelin, 7; Andy Malloy, 3; Battling Johnson, 1; One-Punch Hancock, 1.

Draw: Andy Malloy, 20.

1916

Date	Opponent	Result	Rounds
Jan.	Boston Bearcat, Ogden	KO	1
Feb.	Johnny Sudenberg, Ely, Nev.	KO	2
Feb. 21	Jack Downey, Salt Lake City	KO	2
Mar. 9	Cyril Kohn, Provo, Utah	KO	4
Apr. 8	Joe Bond, Ely, Nev.	W	10
May 3	Terry Keller, Ogden	W	10
May 17	Dan Ketchell, Provo, Utah	KO	3
May	George Christian, Price, Utah	KO	1
June	Bob York, Price, Utah	KO	4
June 24	Andre Anderson, New York	ND	10
July 8	Wild Bert Kenny, New York	ND	10
July 14	John L. Johnson, New York	ND	10
Sept. 28	Young Hector, Salida	KO	3
Oct. 7	Terry Keller, Ely, Nev.	W	10
Oct. 16	Dick Gilbert, Salt Lake City	W	10

1917

Date	Opponent	Result	Rounds
Feb. 13	Jim Flynn, Murray, Utah	KO by	1
Mar. 28	Willie Meehan, Oakland	L	4

Apr.	11—Al Norton, Oakland	D	4
May	21—Al Norton, Oakland	D	4
July	25—Willie Meehan, San Francisco	W	4
Aug.	1—Al. Norton, San Francisco	KO	1
Aug.	10—Willie Meehan, San Francisco	D	4
Sept.	7—Willie Meehan, San Francisco	D	4
Sept.	19—Charley Miller, Oakland	KO	1
Sept.	26—Bob McAllister, Oakland	W	4
Oct.	2—Gunboat Smith, San Francisco	W	4
Oct.	16—Gunboat Smith, San Francisco	ND	4
Nov.	2—Carl Morris, San Francisco	W	4

1918

Jan.	24—Homer Smith, Racine	KO	1
Feb.	4—Carl Morris, Buffalo	WF	6
Feb.	14—Jim Flynn, Fort Sheridan	KO	1
Feb.	25—Bill Brennan, Milwaukee	KO	6
Mar.	16—Fred Saddy, Memphis	KO	1
Mar.	25—Tom Riley, Joplin	KO	1
May	3—Billy Miske, St. Paul	ND	10
May	22—Dan Ketchell, Excelsior Sprg.	KO	2
May	29—Arthur Pelkey, Denver	KO	1
July	1—Kid McCarthy, Tulsa	KO	1
July	4—Bob Devere, Joplin	KO	1
July	6—Porky Flynn, Atlanta	KO	1
July	27—Fred Fulton, Harrison	KO	1
Aug.	17—Terry Keller, Dayton	KO	5
Sept.	13—Willie Meehan, San Francisco	L	4
Sept.	14—Jack Moran, Reno	KO	1
Nov.	6—Battling Levinsky, Phila.	KO	3
Nov.	18—Porky Flynn, Philadelphia	KO	1
Nov.	28—Billy Miske, Philadelphia	ND	6
Dec.	16—Carl Morris, New Orleans	KO	1
Dec.	20—Clay Turner, New York	Exh.	4
Dec.	30—Gunboat Smith, Buffalo	KO	2

1919

Jan.	22—Big Jack Hickey, Harrisburg	KO	1
Jan.	23—Kid Harris, Reading, Pa.	KO	1
Jan.	29—Kid Henry, Easton, Pa.	KO	1
Feb.	13—Eddy Smith, Altoona, Pa.	KO	1
Apr.	2—Tony Drake, New Haven	KO	1
May	1—Terry Keller, Wash., D. C.	Exh.	3
July	4—Jess Willard, Toledo, O.	KO	3
	Won heavyweight championship		
Aug.	24—One Round Garrison, St. Louis	Exh.	4

1920

Mar.	5—Terry Keller, Los Angeles	Exh.	3
July	2—Two spar. pards., Denver, Col.	KO	
Sept.	6—*Billy Miske, Benton Harbor	KO	3

Dec. 14—*Bill Brennan, N. Y. ______ KO 12
*Title bout.

1921

July 2—*Georges Carpentier, Jer. Cy. ______ KO 4
*Title bout.

1922

July 18—‡Elziar Rioux, Montreal ______ Exh. KO 1
July 19—Jack Renault, Ottawa, Can. ______ Exh. 3
Sept. 4—Jack Thompson, Mich. City ______ Exh. 2
Sept. 7—Andre Anderson, Mich. City ______ Exh. 2
Oct. 7—Jack Thompson, Boston ______ Exh. 3
‡Dempsey stopped two other men in one round each in the same ring.

1923

July 4—*Tommy Gibbons, Shelby, Mont. ______ W 15
Sept. 14—*Luis Firpo, New York ______ KO 2
*Title bout.

1924

Feb. 10—Dutch Seifert, Memphis ______ Exh. KO 1
Feb. 11—Martin Burke, New Or. ______ Exh. 2
Feb. 11—Tommy Marvin, New Or. ______ Exh. KO 2
June 3—Rock Stragmalia, Los Angeles ______ Exh. KO 2
June 3—Joe Ryan, Los Angeles ______ Exh. KO 1
June 3—Eli Stanton, Los Angeles ______ Exh. KO 1

1925

Engaged in 8 exhibitions, KO'd Bill Larne, 2, and Ed Warner, 2.

1926

Feb. 8, knocked out Jack League, Tony Catalina, Cowboy Warner and Marty Cuyler, 1 round each, Memphis (exh.). Took on 6 opponents.
Feb. 12, boxed six opponents, knocking out four (exh.).
Sept. 23—Gene Tunney, Philadelphia ______ L 10
(Lost heavyweight title)

1927

July 21—Jack Sharkey, N. Y. ______ KO 7
Sept. 22—Gene Tunney, Chicago, Ill. ______ L 10
(Heavyweight title bout)
The second Tunney fight ended Dempsey's active ring career.

1931

Aug. 19—Jack Beasley, Reno, Nev. ______ KO 2
Aug. 24—Big Bill Hartwell, Port., Ore. ______ KO 1
Aug. 24—Dave McRae, Portland, Ore. ______ KO 1
Aug. 24—Denny Lenhart, Port., Ore. ______ Exh. 2
Aug. 24—Bob Mariels, Port., Ore. ______ Exh. 2
Aug 26—Denny Lenhart, Seattle ______ Exh. 2

Aug.	26—Bob Frazier, Seattle	Exh.	1
Aug.	26—Red Tingley, Seattle	Exh.	1
Aug.	28—Big Tom Sawyer, Vancouver	KO	1
Aug.	28—Tiny Lamar, Vancouver	Exh.	1
Aug.	28—Del Wolfe, Vancouver	Exh.	2
Aug.	31—Elgin Taylor, Spokane	KO	1
Aug.	31—Dee Richmond, Spokane	KO	1
Aug.	31—Big Bill Neering, Spokane	KO	1
Aug.	31—Tony Talerico, Spokane	KO	1
Aug.	31—Cyclone Thompson, Spokane	Exh.	2
Sept.	2—Tom Moore, Aberdeen	KO	1
Sept.	2—Al Devaney, Aberdeen	KO	1
Sept.	2—Denny Lenhart, Aberdeen	Exh.	2
Sept.	4—Jimmy Byrnes, Eugene, Ore.	Exh.	
Sept.	7—Eddie Burns, Reno, Nev.	Exh.	2
Sept.	7—Sam Baker, Reno, Nev.	Exh.	1
Sept.	7—Red Tingley, Reno, Nev.	KO	2
Sept.	10—Marine Raniere, Tacoma	Exh.	1
Sept.	10—George Richard, Tacoma	Exh.	2
Sept.	10—Cyclone Thompson, Tacoma	Exh.	1
Sept.	10—Wayne Pitts, Tacoma	Exh.	1
Sept.	14—Sailor Smith, Rock Spgs., Wyo.	KO	1
Sept.	14—Joe Ferguson, Rock Spgs.	Exh.	2
Sept.	14—Del Baxter, Rk. Spgs., Wyo.	Exh.	2
Sept.	14—Bud Doyle, Rk. Spgs., Wyo.	Exh.	2
Sept.	15—Jackie Silvers, Salt Lake City	Exh. KO	1
Sept.	15—Bill Longston, Salt Lake City	Exh. KO	1
Sept.	16—Del Baxter, Logan, Utah	Exh.	1
Sept.	16—Batt. Lamoreaux, Logan, Utah	Exh.	1
Sept.	16—Cyclone Workman, Logan, Utah	Exh.	1
Sept.	16—George Nelson, Logan, Utah	Exh.	1
Sept.	17—Jack Smith, Boise, Idaho	Exh.	1
Sept.	17—Hank Potter, Boise, Idaho	Exh.	1
Sept.	17—Lewis O'Connely, Boise, Idaho	Exh.	2
Sept.	17—Batt. Lamoreaux, Boise, Idaho	Exh.	1
Sept.	17—Mick. McCafferty, Boise, Idaho	Exh.	1
Nov.	6—Jack Riley, Provo, Utah	KO	1
Nov.	6—Jack Carroll, Provo, Utah	Exh.	
Nov.	6—Del Baxter, Provo, Utah	Exh.	
Nov.	9—Tommy Davenport, Des Moines, Ia.	W	2
Nov.	9—Elijah Lee, Des Moines, Ia.	KO	1
Nov.	9—Happy Shade, Des Moines, Ia.	W	3
Nov.	11—Bearcat Wright, Omaha	W	4
Nov.	13—Pete Wistort, Moline, Ill.	W	2
Nov.	13—Geo. Neron, Moline, Ill.	W	2
Nov.	18—Jack Roper, Kan. City, Mo.	Exh.	2
Nov.	18—Charlie Belanger, Kansas City, Mo.	Exh.	2
Nov.	20—Angus Snyder, Wichita, Kan.	KO	1
Nov.	23—Babe Hunt, Tulsa, Okla.	Exh. ND	4
Nov.	27—Rufino Alvarez, Phoenix	KO	1
Nov.	27—Ernie Musick, Phoenix	KO	1

Nov.	27—Jimmy Long, Phoenix	KO	1
Dec.	4—Johnny Korando, Fargo, N. D.	KO	1
Dec.	4—Swede Grantsburg, Fargo	KO	1
Dec.	4—Charley Retzlaff, Fargo	Exh.	1
Dec.	7—Pat McLaughlin, Duluth	Exh. W	1
Dec.	7—Szymka Zabuil, Duluth	Exh. W	1
Dec.	7—Charley Retzlaff, Duluth	W	
Dec.	12—Art Lasky, St. Paul, Minn.	W	2
Dec.	12—Jack Roper, St. Paul, Minn.	W	1
Dec.	12—Angus McDonald, St. Paul	W	1
Dec.	15—Charley Belanger, Winnipeg	Exh.	2
Dec.	15—Stan Trojack, Winnipeg	Exh.	1
Dec.	15—Angus McDonald, Winnipeg	Exh.	1
Dec.	18—Herman Raschke, Sioux Falls	KO	1
Dec.	18—Louis Zack, Sious Falls, S. D.	W	2
Dec.	18—Chas. Pailson, Sioux Falls, S. D.	KO	1

1932

Feb.	1—Bad News Johnson, Stockton, Cal.	KO	3
Feb.	1—Wally Hunt, Stockton, Cal.	KO	1
Feb.	8—Buck Everett, Milwaukee	W	2
Feb.	8—Jack Roper, Milwaukee	W	2
Feb.	11—K. O. Christner, Cleveland	KO	3
Feb.	15—George Kohler, Flint	KO	1
Feb.	15—Pat McLaughlin, Flint	KO	1
Feb.	18—King Levinsky, Chicago	Exh.	4
Feb.	23—Frankie Wine, Louisville, Ky.	Exh.	4
Feb.	29—Jack Phillips, Dayton, O.	KO	1
Feb.	29—Pat Sullivan, Dayton, O.	KO	1
Mar.	3—George Trenkle, Cincinnati	Exh.	2
Mar.	3—Ray Vanzke, Cincinnati	Exh.	2
Mar.	7—Johnny Chick, Columbus	KO	1
Mar.	7—Eddie Anderson, Columbus	KO	1
Mar.	10—Hank Hankinson, Akron, O.	KO	2
Mar.	10—Tiny Powell, Akron, O.	KO	2
Mar.	12—Tim Charles, Toledo, O.	Exh. W	2
Mar.	12—Jack O'Dowd, Toledo, O.	Exh. W	2
Mar.	16—Big Ed Williams, Clarksburg, W. Va.	KO	1
Mar.	16—Freddie Taylor, Clarksburg	KO	1
Mar.	18—Billy Miles, Huntington, W. Va.	KO	1
Mar.	18—Jack Kearns, Hunt'gt'n, W. Va.	W	2
Mar.	21—Joe Doctor, Toronto, Ont.	W	4
Mar.	31—Babe Hunt, Detroit	Exh.	4

1940

July	1—Cowboy Luttrell, Atlanta	KO	2
July	15—Bull Curry, Detroit	KO	2
July	29—Ellis Bashara, Charlotte, N. C.	KO	2

TB	KO	WD	WF	D	LD	LF	KOBY	ND	NC
81	49	10	1	8	6	0	1	6	0

Appendix III

RECEIPTS AND ATTENDANCE FOR DEMPSEY'S MAJOR CHAMPIONSHIP FIGHTS

DEMPSEY-WILLARD FIGHT

Date—July 4, 1919.
Place—Bay View Park Arena, Toledo, Ohio, on shores of Maumee Bay.
Distance—Scheduled for 12 rounds.
Bout ended in third—Willard called a halt during the intermission between third and fourth rounds.
Official attendance—19,650.
Official receipts—$452,224.
Government tax—$67,680.
Net—$384,544.
Charity—Seven percent of net to city of Toledo—$28,751.25.
Purse—To Willard—$100,000 guarantee.
To Dempsey—$27,500 guarantee.
Construction of arena—$100,000.
Expenses for fight—Total—$307,500.
Publicity—$17,500.
Gross expenses—$325,000.
Profit—$85,732.16.
Promoters—Tex Rickard and his partner, Frank Flournoy.

The above are the official figures given to the press by Rickard.

The arena was constructed to seat 97,000. After the bout the entire arena was sold to the American House Wrecking Company for $25,000, the highest bidder. The plant had a total of 2,000,000 feet of lumber.

Officials—Ollie Pecord, Toledo, Referee. He was chosen by Major A. Drexel Biddle, Chairman of the Navy and Civilian Board of Boxing Control.

Tex Rickard and Biddle were chosen as judges and Jack Skelly of Yonkers, N.Y., was selected as alternate referee. The timekeeper was Warren Barbour of New York.

Willard's seconds were Sergeant Walter Moynahan, Jack Hemple, and Ray Archer.

Dempsey's seconds were Jack Kearns, Bill Tate, Joe Chip, and Tom Bodkin.

DEMPSEY-CARPENTIER FIGHT

Date—July 2, 1921.
Place—Boyle's Thirty Acres, Jersey City, N. J.
Scheduled distance—12 rounds.
Official attendance—80,183.
Official gross—$1,789,238.
Dempsey's share (guaranteed)—$300,000.
Dempsey's share (from movies)—$4,000.
Carpentier's share (guaranteed)—$200,000.
Promoted by Tex Rickard.

DEMPSEY-FIRPO FIGHT

Date—Sept. 14, 1923.
Place—Polo Grounds, New York, N. Y.
Scheduled distance—15 rounds
Official attendance—82,000.
Official gross—$1,188,603.
Federal tax—$180,074.80.
State tax—$57,197.
Dempsey's share (including movies)—$509,000.
Firpo's share—$156,250.
Promoted by Tex Rickard

TUNNEY-DEMPSEY FIRST FIGHT

Date—Sept. 23, 1926.
Place—Sesquicentennial Stadium, Philadelphia, Pa.
Scheduled distance—10 rounds.
Official attendance—120,757.
Official gross—$1,895,733.
Government tax—$189,000.
State tax—$98,000.
Rental of stadium—$200,000.
Sesquicentennial share—$200,000.
Dempsey's share—$717,000.
Tunney's share—$200,000.
Promoted by Tex Rickard.

TUNNEY-DEMPSEY SECOND FIGHT

Date—Sept. 22, 1927.
Place—Soldiers' Field, Chicago, Ill.
Scheduled distance—10 rounds.
Official attendance—104,943.
Official gross receipts—$2,658,660.
Net receipts—$2,151,134.57.
Tunney's share—$990,445.
Dempsey's share—$425,000, plus $25,000 from film rights.

Federal tax—$265,866.
Illinois state tax—$241,659.43.
Soldiers' Field rental—$100,000.
Expenses listed by promoter Tex Rickard—$150,000.
Promoter Rickard's profit—$551,134.57.

Appendix IV

JACK DEMPSEY'S RING EARNINGS

Receipts at Boxing Shows in Which the Manassa Mauler Appeared from 1919 to 1932

Date	Winner	Loser	Place	Share	Receipts	Movies
Sept. 22, 1927	Tunney	Dempsey	Chicago	$425,000	$2,658,660	$25,000
Sept. 23, 1926	Tunney	Dempsey	Philadelphia	717,000	1,895,733	6,000
July 2, 1921	Dempsey	Carpentier	Jersey City	300,000	1,789,238	4,000
Sept. 6, 1920	Dempsey	Miske	Benton Harbor	55,000	134,904	———
July 4, 1923	Dempsey	Gibbons	Shelby	250,000	201,485	———
July 4, 1919	Dempsey	Willard	Toledo	27,500	452,224	6,000
July 21, 1927	Dempsey	Sharkey	New York	252,759	1,083,530	6,000
Dec. 14, 1920	Dempsey	Brennan	New York	100,000	162,760	8,000
Sept. 14, 1923	Dempsey	Firpo	New York	509,000	1,188,603	30,000
Feb. 18, 1932	No decision	King Levinsky vs. Dempsey		33,000	74,199	———
First refereeing tour				$259,949	371,379	———
Second refereeing tour				291,842	471,560	———
Third refereeing tour				246,066	492,132	———

Total share from boxing bouts, including his referee tours up to 1934 ———— $3,486,116

Total including movie rights for the same period ———— $3,541,116

Since 1935 Dempsey has earned several million. He estimates this sum for the past 35 years to be around $4,000,000 for refereeing boxing and wrestling, radio appearances, and lectures including several big business ventures. Total for all: ———— $10,568,114

Appendix V

DEMPSEY'S MEASUREMENTS IN MAJOR CONTESTS

DEMPSEY	*vs.*	FULTON

At Harrison, New Jersey, July 27, 1918, Dempsey won by a knockout in the first round.

23 years	Age	27 years
188 lbs.	Weight	208 lbs.
6 ft. 1 in.	Height	6 ft. 5½ in.
78 in.	Reach	84 ½ in.
44 in.	Chest (normal)	43 in.
48 in.	Chest (expanded)	47 ½ in.
34 in.	Waist	35 in.
17 ½ in.	Neck	18 in.
8 ½ in.	Wrist	9 in.
23 in.	Thigh	21 in.
15 in.	Calf	13 ½ in.
13 ½ in.	Biceps	15 in.
9 in.	Ankle	7 ½ in.

DEMPSEY	*vs.*	WILLARD

At Toledo, Ohio, July 4, 1919, Dempsey won in the third round. Willard quit during the intermission between the third and fourth rounds.

DEMPSEY		WILLARD
24 years	Age	37 years
191 lbs.	Weight	245 lbs.
6 ft. 1 in.	Height	6 ft. 6¼ in.
77 in.	Reach	83 ½ in.
42 in.	Chest (normal)	46 in.
46 in.	Chest (expanded)	49 ½ in.
33 in.	Waist	38 in.
16 ½ in.	Neck	17 ½ in.
9 in.	Wrist	10 in.
23 in.	Thigh	27 ½ in.
15 in.	Calf	17 ½ in.
9 in.	Ankle	10 in.
14 ½ in.	Forearm	14 in.
16 ¼ in.	Biceps	17 ½ in.

DEMPSEY	*vs.*	MISKE

At Benton Harbor, Michigan, September 6, 1920, Dempsey won by a knockout in the third round.

25 years	Age	26 years
188 lbs.	Weight	175 ½ lbs.
6 ft. 1 in.	Height	6 ft. 1 in.
78 in.	Reach	77 in.
39 in.	Chest (normal)	39 in.
44 in.	Chest (expanded)	44 in.
17 in.	Neck	17 ½ in.
20 ½ in.	Shoulders	20 ½ in.
32 in.	Waist	33 in.
15 in.	Biceps	15 ½ in.
14 ½ in.	Forearm	13 ½ in.
8 in.	Wrist	7 ¼ in.
21 in.	Thigh	22 ½ in.
14 ½ in.	Calf	15 ½ in.
8 ½ in.	Ankle	9 in.

DEMPSEY	*vs.*	BRENNAN

December 14, 1920, Madison Square Garden, New York City. Dempsey won by a knockout in the 12th round.

25 years	Age	28 years
187 ½ lbs.	Weight	197 lbs.
6 ft. 1 in.	Height	6 ft. 1½ in.

DEMPSEY		BRENNAN
8 in.	Wrist	8 in.
8 ½ in.	Ankle	8 ½ in.
17 in.	Neck	17 in.
15 in.	Biceps	15 in.
39 in.	Chest (normal)	42 in.
44 in.	Chest (expanded)	45 in.
29 in.	Waist	30 ½ in.
78 in.	Reach	77 in.
23 in.	Thigh	23 in.
18 in.	Calf	18 in.

DEMPSEY *vs.* CARPENTIER

At Boyle's Thirty Acres, Jersey City, New Jersey, July 2, 1921, Dempsey won by a knockout in the fourth round.

DEMPSEY		CARPENTIER
26 years	Age	27 years
188 lbs.	Weight	175 lbs.
6 ft. 1 in.	Height	5 ft. 11 in.
78 in.	Reach	76 in.
16 ½ in.	Neck	15 ½ in.
42 in.	Chest (normal)	40 in.
46 in.	Chest (expanded)	44 in.
16 ¼ in.	Biceps	15 ¾ in.
14 ¼ in.	Forearm	13 in.
9 ¼ in.	Wrist	8 ¾ in.
32 in.	Waist	29 in.
23 in.	Thigh	22 in.
15 in.	Calf	14 ½ in.
9 in.	Ankle	8 ¾ in.

DEMPSEY *vs.* GIBBONS

July 4, 1923, Shelby Montana. Dempsey won a 15-round decision.

DEMPSEY		GIBBONS
28 years	Age	32 years
188 lbs.	Weight	175 ½ lbs.
6 ft. 1 in.	Height	5 ft. 10 in.
78 in.	Reach	74 in.
17 in.	Neck	17 in.
41 in.	Chest (normal)	41 in.
44 in.	Chest (expanded)	44 ½ in.
32 ½ in.	Waist	35 in.
15 in.	Biceps	14 in.
12 ½ in.	Forearm	12 ½ in.
8 ¼ in.	Wrist	9 in.
22 in.	Thigh	22 ½ in.
15 in.	Calf	14 ½ in.
9 in.	Ankle	9 ½ in.

DEMPSEY *vs.* FIRPO

At the Polo Grounds, New York City, September 14, 1923, Dempsey won by a knockout in the second round.

DEMPSEY		FIRPO
28 years	Age	26 years
192 ½ lbs.	Weight	216 ½ lbs.
6 ft. 1 in.	Height	6 ft. 2½ in.
78 in.	Reach	79 in.
17 in.	Neck	17 in.
15 in.	Biceps	13 ½ in.
41 in.	Chest (normal)	44 in.
44 ½ in.	Chest (expanded)	48 ½ in.
32 ½ in.	Waist	36 ½ in.
8 ¼ in.	Wrist	8 ¼ in.
22 in.	Thigh	23 ¾ in.
15 in.	Calf	15 in.
9 in.	Ankle	9 ½ in.

DEMPSEY *vs.* TUNNEY

At Sesquicentennial Stadium, Philadelphia, Pennsylvania, September, 23, 1926, Dempsey lost the heavyweight title via ten-round decision.

DEMPSEY		TUNNEY
31 years	Age	29 years
190 lbs.	Weight	192 lbs.
6 ft. 1 in.	Height	6 ft. ½ in.
78 in.	Reach	77 in.
9 in.	Wrist	9 in.
13 in.	Forearm	13 ½ in.
14 ½ in.	Biceps	14 ½ in.
40 ½ in.	Chest (normal)	42 in.
44 in.	Chest (expanded)	45 in.
33 in.	Waist	34 ½ in.
16 ½ in.	Neck	17 in.
22 in.	Thigh	22 in.
16 in.	Calf	15 ½ in.
9 in.	Ankle	9 in.

DEMPSEY	*vs.*	SHARKEY

At Yankee Stadium, New York City, July 21, 1927, Dempsey won by a knockout in the seventh round.

32 years	Age	24 years
194 ½ lbs.	Weight	196 lbs.
6 ft. 1 in.	Height	6 ft.
78 in.	Reach	72 in.
40 in.	Chest (normal)	42 in.
44 ½ in.	Chest (expanded)	46 in.
32 in.	Waist	34 ½ in.
14 in.	Biceps	13 in.
14 in.	Forearm	12 in.
21 ½ in.	Thigh	23 ½ in.
15 ½ in.	Calf	16 ½ in.
9 ½ in.	Ankle	9 ½ in.
16 in.	Neck	16 ½ in.
9 in.	Wrist	8 in.

TUNNEY	*vs.*	DEMPSEY

At Soldiers' Field, Chicago, Illinois, September 22, 1927, Dempsey lost via decision in ten rounds.

30 years	Age	32 years
189 ½ lbs.	Weight	192 ½ lbs.
6 ft. ½ in.	Height	6 ft. 1 in.
76 ½ in.	Reach	78 in.
17 in.	Neck	16 ½ in.
41 in.	Chest (normal)	40 ½ in.
44 in.	Chest (expanded)	44 ¾ in.
34 in.	Waist	33 in.
14 in.	Biceps	14 ½ in.
13 ½ in.	Forearm	13 in.
23 in.	Thigh	22 in.
16 in.	Calf	15 ½ in.
9 in.	Ankle	9 in.
8 in.	Wrist	9 in.

DEMPSEY	*vs.*	LEVINSKY

At Chicago Stadium, Chicago, Illinois, February 18, 1932. No decision.

DEMPSEY		LEVINSKY
36 years	Age	22 years
190 lbs.	Weight	196 ½ lbs.
6 ft. 1 in.	Height	5 ft. 11½ in.
77 in.	Reach	71 in.
16 ½ in.	Neck	16 in.
41 ½ in.	Chest (normal)	42 in.
45 ¾ in.	Chest (expanded)	44 in.
33 in.	Waist	33 in.
9 ¼ in.	Wrist	8 in.
13 ½ in.	Forearm	13 in.
9 ¼ in.	Ankle	9 ½ in.
16 in.	Calf	16 in.
22 ½ in.	Thigh	20 in.

Appendix VI

HEAVYWEIGHT TITLE SHIFTS

One frequently hears the expression in America, "Tom, Dick, or Harry," which carries the implication that those are the most common names among the English-speaking people. That may be true, but not in boxing.

No Dick or Harry ever ruled the roost as king of the heavyweights, but there was a Tom. He was a Canadian-born fighter who became an American citizen. His full fighting name was Tommy Burns but he was christened Noah Brusso.

It is interesting to scan the list of world heavyweight champions from John L. Sullivan to Joe Frazier and note the names of the titleholders. The *J* has it all over the others, with 12 out of 23 so listed —John L. Sullivan, James J. Corbett, James J. Jeffries, Jack Johnson, Jess Willard, Jack Dempsey, James Tunney, Jack Sharkey, James J. Braddock, Joe Louis, Jersey Joe Walcott, and Joe Frazier.

Following are the championship changes from the day Corbett dethroned Sullivan to the present:

September 7, 1892—James J. Corbett knocked out John L. Sullivan at New Orleans, 21 rounds.

March 17, 1897—Bob Fitzsimmons knocked out James J. Corbett at Carson City, Nev., 14 rounds.

June 9, 1899—James J. Jeffries knocked out Bob Fitzsimmons at Coney Island, N.Y., 11 rounds.

Jeffries announced his retirement in 1904. The title was passed on to Marvin Hart by Jeffries after Hart had stopped Jack Root in 12 rounds in a bout refereed by Jeffries. It took place July 3, 1905, at Reno, Nev.

February 23, 1906—Tommy Burns defeated Marvin Hart at Los Angeles, 20 rounds.

December 26, 1908—Jack Johnson stopped Tommy Burns at Sydney, Australia, 14 rounds. Police stopped the bout.

April 5, 1915—Jess Willard knocked out Jack Johnson at Havana, Cuba, 26 rounds.

July 4, 1919—Jack Dempsey knocked out Jess Willard at Toledo, Ohio, 3 rounds.

September 23, 1926—Gene Tunney outpointed Jack Dempsey at

Philadelphia, 10 rounds.

Tunney announced his retirement in 1928, after defeating Dempsey (1927, Chicago, 10 rounds) and Tom Heeney (1928, New York, KO, 11 rounds).

June 12, 1930—In the final elimination to decide Tunney's successor, Max Schmeling of Germany won on a foul in a bout with Jack Sharkey at New York City, 4 rounds.

June 21, 1932—Jack Sharkey defeated Max Schmeling at Long Island City, N.Y., 15 rounds.

June 29, 1933—Primo Carnera of Italy knocked out Jack Sharkey at Long Island City, N.Y., 6 rounds.

June 14, 1934—Max Baer knocked out Primo Carnera at Long Island City, N.Y., 11 rounds.

June 13, 1935—Jimmy Braddock defeated Max Baer at Long Island City, N.Y., 15 rounds.

June 22, 1937—Joe Louis knocked out Jimmy Braddock at Chicago, 8 rounds.

Joe Louis retired on March 1, 1949, as an undefeated champion. Several tournaments were staged and Ezzard Charles, on June 22, 1949, defeated Jersey Joe Walcott for the NBA title at Chicago, 15 rounds.

After several bouts in which he triumphed, Charles defended his NBA crown in Buffalo, N.Y., where on August 15, 1950, he knocked out Freddy Beshore, 14 rounds. With that victory he gained universal recognition as the world titleholder.

July 18, 1951—Jersey Joe Walcott knocked out Ezzard Charles at Pittsburgh, 7 rounds.

September 23, 1952—Rocky Marciano knocked out Jersey Joe Walcott at Philadelphia, 13 rounds.

On April 27, 1956, undefeated champion Marciano announced his retirement.

November 30, 1956—Floyd Patterson knocked out Archie Moore at Chicago, 5 rounds, to win the vacant crown.

June 26, 1959—Ingemar Johansson of Sweden knocked out Floyd Patterson at New York City, 3 rounds.

June 20, 1960—Floyd Patterson became the first man to regain the heavyweight title, doing so by his kayo of Ingemar Johansson at New York City, 5 rounds.

September 25, 1962—Sonny Liston knocked out Floyd Patterson at Chicago, 1 round.

February 25, 1964—Cassius Clay knocked out Sonny Liston at Miami Beach, 7 rounds.

On February 3, 1970, Clay, following three years of inactivity because of his refusal to be drafted into the armed forces, announced his retirement.

February 16, 1970—Joe Frazier kayoed Jimmy Ellis at New York City, 5 rounds, to win the vacant title.

Appendix VII

RATING THE HEAVYWEIGHTS

Recent years have produced many power hitters among the heavyweights; but in terms of percentages, there are far fewer now than were in evidence when I started my career as a sportswriter in 1906 and for many years thereafter. I do not belittle the crop that came forth after World War II, but if a comparison were made, I should give my vote to those who were in the fold before.

The old boxer was a hardy soul, a tough fighter who carried into the ring explosive punching power, and who fought tougher fighters than have been available in the years following the retirements of top pugilists like Joe Louis and Rocky Marciano.

For every power-hitting heavyweight and scientific boxer in that division in the last few years, we've had only a few since Louis's retirement who possessed the qualities that brought fame to those who preceded the Brown Bomber.

Let's take a peep at just a few of the names that stand out in the heavyweight sector of the past—James J. Jeffries, Jack Dempsey, Tom Sharkey, Bob Fitzsimmons, Bob Armstrong, Sam Langford, and Gunboat Smith. Giants all! Think of what a promoter could do with fighters like that today!

Looking over the field of heavyweight champions from John L. Sullivan to Joe Frazier, we find that the majority of those who held the crown were good hitters. A few possessed the combination of hitting and cleverness.

Who was the hardest hitter in the group?

Many give that honor to Dempsey, but as many, I venture, hand the honor to Louis, Jeffries, or Marciano.

Who among the large field possessed the best ring cleverness?

Of the answers I've received to that query, Gene Tunney comes in first. But Corbett, with his science, stamina, and speed, is a close second.

In general ability, the honors go to Jack Johnson. He received more votes than all the other fighters who were mentioned.

A fighter who relies almost wholly on hard punching doesn't get as far as one who possesses hitting power and cleverness. He's like a long-ball hitter in baseball who can do little else; when he connects he is likely to blast the ball out of the park, but between those occasional wallops he strikes out often, is a poor fielder, and jams up many plays by inept baserunning. Boxing, like baseball, calls for more than power hitting for headline recognition.

Here is my resume of the finest assets of men who ruled the roost in the heavyweight division:

Best Boxer—James J. Corbett
Fastest Boxer—James J. Corbett
Best All-Around—Jack Johnson
Best Uppercut—Jack Johnson
Best Defensive—Jack Johnson
Best Counter Puncher—Jack Johnson
Most Crafty—Jack Johnson
Best at Feinting—Jack Johnson
Best Left and Hitter—James J. Jeffries
Best Knockout Puncher—Bob Fitzsimmons
Best Hooker—Bob Fitzsimmons
Best Body Puncher—Bob Fitzsimmons
Best Heart Puncher—Jack Dempsey
Best Infighter—Jack Dempsey
Roughest Fighter—Jack Dempsey
Best Two-Handed Hitter—Jack Dempsey
Smartest Boxer—Gene Tunney
Best Jabber—Gene Tunney
Best Conditioned—Gene Tunney
Best Straight Right—Joe Louis
Best Finisher—Joe Louis
Best One-Punch Hitter—Rocky Marciano

Appendix VIII

MEASUREMENTS OF HEAVYWEIGHT CHAMPIONS

Compiled from Official Weigh-In Records When They Won Title

	John L. Sullivan	James J. Corbett	Bob Fitz- simmons	James J. Jeffries	Tommy Burns	Jack Johnson
Height	5 ft. 10¼ in.	6 ft. 1 in.	5 ft. 11¾ in.	6 ft. 2½ in.	5 ft. 7 in.	6 ft. ¼ in.
Weight	200 lbs.	184 lbs.	172 lbs.	225 lbs.	179 lbs.	222 lbs.
Reach	74 in.	73 in.	71¾ in.	76½ in.	74½ in.	74 in.
Chest, Nor.	43 in.	38 in.	41 in.	43 in.	40 in.	37½ in.
Chest, Exp.	48 in.	42 in.	44 in.	48½ in.	43¾ in.	42¾ in.
Waist	36 in.	33 in.	32 in.	35 in.	33 in.	36 in.
Biceps	16¼ in.	14½ in.	12 in.	16 in.	14½ in.	16 in.
Neck	18 in.	17 in.	15 in.	18¼ in.	16 in.	17½ in.
Wrist	8 in.	6½ in.	7½ in.	7¾ in.	7¼ in.	10½ in.
Calf	16 in.	14½ in.	13½ in.	17 in.	16½ in.	15 in.
Ankle	9 in.	8¼ in.	8¼ in.	10 in.	8¼ in.	9½ in.
Thigh	24 in.	21 in.	20 in.	25 in.	22 in.	22½ in.
Fist	14 in.	12¾ in.	12½ in.	13½ in.	12 in.	14 in.
Forearm	13 in.	11½ in.	11½ in.	13½ in.	13 in.	14½ in.

	Jess Willard	Jack Dempsey	Gene Tunney	Max Schmeling	Jack Sharkey	Primo Carnera
Height	6 ft. 6¼ in.	6 ft. 1 in.	6 ft. ½ in.	6 ft. 1 in.	6 ft.	6 ft. 5¾ in.
Weight	252 lbs.	191 lbs.	192 lbs.	188 lbs.	205 lbs.	267 lbs.
Reach	83 in.	77 in.	77 in.	76 in.	74½ in.	85½ in.
Chest, Nor.	46 in.	42 in.	42 in.	43 in.	40½ in.	48 in.
Chest, Exp.	49½ in.	46 in.	45 in.	47 in.	45½ in.	54 in.
Waist	35½ in.	33 in.	34½ in.	33¼ in.	34½ in.	38 in.
Biceps	17½ in.	16¼ in.	14½ in.	16 in.	14½ in.	18½ in.
Neck	17½ in.	16½ in.	17 in.	17½ in.	17 in.	20 in.
Wrist	10 in.	9 in.	9 in.	8 in.	7¾ in.	9½ in.
Calf	17½ in.	15 in.	15½ in.	16 in.	16 in.	20 in.
Ankle	10½ in.	9 in.	9 in.	10 in.	10¼ in.	11½ in.
Thigh	26 in.	23 in.	22 in.	23½ in.	24¾ in.	30 in.
Fist	14 in.	11¼ in.	11¼ in.	12 in.	12¾ in.	14¾ in.
Forearm	14 in.	14½ in.	13½ in.	12¾ in.	15¾ in.	16 in.

	Max Baer	Jimmy Braddock	Joe Louis	Ezzard Charles	Joe Walcott	Rocky Marciano
Height	6 ft. 2½ in.	6 ft. 2 in.	6 ft. 1½ in.	6 ft.	6 ft.	5 ft. 10½ in.
Weight	214 lbs.	197 lbs.	218 lbs.	184½ lbs.	194 lbs.	184 lbs.
Reach	81 in.	75 in.	76 in.	74 in.	74 in.	68 in.
Chest, Nor.	44 in.	41 in.	42 in.	39 in.	40 in.	39 in.
Chest, Exp.	47½ in.	44 in.	45 in.	42 in.	43 in.	42 in.
Waist	32½ in.	34½ in.	36½ in.	33 in.	35 in.	32 in.
Biceps	14½ in.	13 in.	15 in.	15½ in.	16 in.	14 in.
Neck	17½ in.	17 in.	17 in.	16½ in.	17 in.	16¾ in.
Wrist	8 in.	8 in.	8 in.	7 in.	7¾ in.	7½ in.
Calf	15 in.	16 in.	14 in.	13 in.	14 in.	14¾ in.
Ankle	9½ in.	10 in.	10 in.	8½ in.	9¾ in.	10 in.
Thigh	21 in.	22¾ in.	22½ in.	20 in.	21 in.	22 in.
Fist	12 in.	11½ in.	11¾ in.	12 in.	12 in.	11½ in.

	Ingemar Johansson	Floyd Patterson	Sonny Liston	Cassius Clay	Joe Frazier
Height -----	6 ft. ½ in.	6 ft.	6 ft. 1 in.	6 ft. 3 in.	5 ft. 11½ in.
Weight -----	197 lbs.	190 lbs.	212 lbs.	215 lbs.	202 lbs.
Reach -----	72½ in.	71 in.	84 in.	82 in.	73½ in.
Chest, Nor. --	43 in.	40 in.	44 in.	42 in.	42 in.
Chest, Exp. --	45 in.	42 in.	46½ in.	44½ in.	44 in.
Waist -------	34 in.	32½ in.	33 in.	34 in.	34 in.
Biceps -----	16½ in.	14¼ in.	16½ in.	15 in.	15 in.
Neck ------	17 in.	17 in.	17½ in.	17 in.	17½ in.
Wrist ------	7 in.	6 in.	8½ in.	7½ in.	7 in.
Calf -------	16 in.	15½ in.	16 in.	17 in.	13 in.
Ankle ------	10 in.	9½ in.	12 in.	9½ in.	11 in.
Thigh -----	24 in.	21½ in.	25½ in.	25 in.	26 in.
Fist -------	13½ in.	12¾ in.	15 in.	12 in.	13 in.
Forearm ----	15 in.	12 in.	14½ in.	13½ in.	13 in.

Hart was named champion in 1905 by James J. Jeffries when the latter retired, but Hart's claim to crown was not universally recognized

OUTSTANDING MEASUREMENTS OF HEAVYWEIGHT CHAMPIONS

Tallest—Jess Willard—6 feet 6¼ inches
Heaviest—Primo Carnera—267 pounds
Biggest reach—Primo Carnera—85½ inches
Normal chest—Primo Carnera—48 inches
Chest expansion—Primo Carnera—6 inches
Biggest waist—Primo Carnera—38 inches
Largest biceps—Primo Carnera—18½ inches

Largest neck—Primo Carnera—20 inches
Largest wrist—Jack Johnson—10½ inches
Largest calf—Primo Carnera—20 inches
Largest ankle—Sonny Liston—12 inches
Largest thigh—Primo Carnera—30 inches
Largest fist—Sonny Liston—15 inches
Largest forearm—Primo Carnera—16 inches

Index